3·21·18

WEAN YOURSELF

Little by little, wean yourself.
This is the gist of what I have to say.

From an embryo, whose nourishment comes in the blood,
move to an infant drinking milk,
to a child on solid food,
to a searcher after wisdom,
to a hunter of more invisible game.

Think how it is to have a conversation with an embryo.
You might say, "The world outside is vast and intricate.
There are wheatfields and mountain passes,
and orchards in bloom.

At night there are millions of galaxies, and in sunlight
the beauty of friends dancing at a wedding."

You ask the embryo why he, or she, stays cooped up
in the dark with eyes closed.
                              Listen to the answer

There is no "other world."
I only know what I've experienced.
You must be hallucinating.

– Rumi

ORBITING THE GIANT HAIRBALL
A Corporate Fool's Guide to Surviving with Grace

Gordon MacKenzie

VIKING
Published by the Penguin Group
Penguin Putnam Inc., 375 Hudson Street,
New York, New York 10014, U.S.A.
Penguin Books Ltd., 27 Wrights Lane,
London W8 5TZ, England
Penguin Books Australia Ltd, Ringwood,
Victoria Australia
Penguing Books Canada Ltd, 10 Alcorn Avenue,
Toronto, Ontario, Canada M4V 3B2
Penguin Group (N.Z.) Ltd, 182-190 Wairau Road,
Auckland 10, New Zealand

Penguin Books Ltd., Registered Offices:
Harmondsworth, Middlesex, England

Published in 1998 by Viking Penguin,
a member of Penguin Putnam Inc.

27 28 29 30 31

Grateful acknowledgement is made for permission to use the following copyrighted material:

Page 3 Reprinted with the permission of Threshold Books, RD 4 Box 600, Putney, VT 05346 from *The Essential Rumi*, translated by Coleman Barks with John Moyne. Copyright © 1995 by Coleman Barks.

Page 47 Reprinted with the permission of Bantam Doubleday Dell Publishing from *The Power of Myth*, by Joseph Campbell with Bill Moyers. Copyright © 1988 by Apostrophe S Productions, Inc., and Alfred der Mark Editions.

Page 89 Reprinted with the permission of Simon & Schuster from *The Matter Myth*, by Paul Davis and John Gribben. Copyright © 1992 by Orion Productions and John Gribbin.

Page 101 Paws, Inc. © 1985 Dist. by Universal Press Syndicate. Reprinted with permission.

Library of Congress Cataloging-in-Publication Data
Mackenzie, Gordon.
Orbiting the giant hairball : a corporate fool's guide to surviving with grace / Gordon MacKenzie.
p. cm.
Originally published: Shawnee Mission, KS : OpusPocus Pub., c1996.
ISBN 0-670-87983-5 (alk. paper)
1. MacKenzie, Gordon—Notebooks, sketchbooks, etc. I. Title.
N6537.M3136A2 1998
650.1—dc21
97-52991

This book is printed on acid-free paper.

Printed in the United States of America
Set in Goudy
Designed by Willoughby Design Group, Kansas City, Missouri

Laurie Rippon
    who heralded this tome-foolery
        into Viking
            before

                zoommmmming off.

                        Thanks.

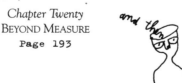

Book Design   Michelle Sonderegger

Graffiti   Meg Cundiff

Paintings and Illustrations   Meg Cundiff *(pages 14, 26, 82, 107, 160)*
                         Susi Lulaki *(pages 34, 54, 68, 198, 218)*
                         Ann Willoughby *(pages 42, 98, 132)*
                         Wendie Collins *(pages 94, 114, 212)*
                         Gordon MacKenzie *(pages 48, 208)*

Photography   Mike Regnier *(pages 62, 142, 154, 192)*

Text   Gordon MacKenzie
                         Meg Cundiff *(pages 82, 83)*

ORBITING THE GIANT HAIRBALL

Chapter One

WHERE HAVE ALL THE GENIUSES GONE?

Groaning under its overload of blacksmith equipment and steel passengers — a menagerie of elephants, crocodiles, Stegosauri, turtles and sundry fantasy creatures — my rusted-out pickup swayed ominously as I gentled it into the school parking lot to a safe stop.

I turned the ignition key to off. The engine obeyed and went silent. The truck became still.

> *"Whew. Made it. The Eagle... Owl... Crow has landed. One more time... without calamity."*

Curious children began milling around the truck. Some noisily reached up to touch the coarsely tethered animals while others, holding back, watched silently. Perhaps a few realized that what was to be the highlight of their day had just arrived: The Diversion. The Disruption. The Hope for Escape, however temporary, from the routine of another day at school.

I loved this! It was — is — what I was made for: disruption of routine. Not pointless disruption. Disruption with purpose. In this case the purpose was to share with grade-school children the experience of transforming flat, cold sheets of steel into animals that were touched with enough spirit and soul as to be almost alive. Sound like magic? You got it.

Magic!

I was here to show the children that the magic of creativity can happen even in the institutional environment where formal learning is supposed to take place.

This was the same sort of disruption I had been creating in the institutional environment of Hallmark Cards, Inc., where I had originally hired on as a sketch artist. Over the years, I had gradually evolved into a self-styled corporate holy man — but more of that later.

Sculpting in steel had already been a passion of mine for four or five years when a colleague at Hallmark asked whether I would be interested in giving a demonstration of my craft to the students of the grade school where his wife served as the cultural arts coordinator (a.k.a. Picture Lady). I accepted the invitation and found it such a delightful experience that I made visiting schools a part of my sculpting adventure for the next several years. A dozen times a year, I'd take a day off from work to make magic with the children.

Arriving early in the morning, I'd set up shop in the school's art room or gymnasium. Most commonly, the schedule had me visit with one grade level at a time, spending about 50 minutes with each.

As I was putting on my welding goggles and scarred leather apron, the teachers would herd the children in, barking orders at them to sit cross-legged on the floor in rows facing the semicircle of sculptures and equipment arranged at one end of the room.

"Chatter! Chatter! Chatter! Chatter! Chatter! Chatter!"

"Quiet, children, quiet."

"Chatter Chatter Chatter Chatter Chatter... "

"Quiet. Joel. Cindy! Quiet. Now!"

"whisper whisper whisper whisper whisper whisper"

"Robert. Shhhhhh!"

"Pam!"

"   "

With the coming of silence, the children's faces took on a certain solemnity. Satisfied that order had been attained, the teachers would retire to the back of the room to lose themselves in grading papers, leaving me, for all practical purposes, alone with the children. I always began with the same introduction:

> "Hi! My name is Gordon MacKenzie and, among other things, I am an artist. I'll bet there are other artists here, too. There have to be with all the beautiful pictures and designs you have hanging in your classrooms and up and down the halls. I couldn't help but notice them when I first got here this morning.

> "Beautiful pictures. They made me feel wonderful! Very energized. So many bright colors and cool shapes. I felt more at home when I saw them because they made me realize there are other artists here, besides me. I'm curious. How many artists are there in the room? Would you please raise your hands?"

The pattern of responses never varied.

First grade:
En mass the children leapt from their chairs, arms waving wildly, eager hands trying to reach the ceiling. Every child was an artist.

Second grade:
About half the kids raised their hands, shoulder high, no higher. The raised hands were still.

Third grade:
At best, 10 kids out of 30 would raise a hand. Tentatively. Self-consciously.

19.

And so on up through the grades. The higher the grade, the fewer children raised their hands. By time I reached sixth grade, no more than one or two did so and then only ever-so-slightly — *guardedly* — their eyes glancing from side to side uneasily, betraying a fear of being identified by the group as a "closet artist."

I would describe to the sixth graders the different responses I had received from the other grade levels. Then I'd ask:

> *"What's going on here? Are all the artists transferring out and going to art school?"*

(Usually, in recognition of my little joke, the students would laugh.)

> *"Uh-uh. I don't think that's it. I'm afraid there's something much more sinister than that at work here. I think what's happening is that you are being tricked out of one of the greatest gifts every one of us receives at birth. That is the gift of being an artist, a creative genius."*

They could reclaim their creative genius, I'd tell the students. It may not be easy, but it will always remain doable. We'll get further into that later on.

The point now is:

> *Every school I visited was participating in the suppression of creative genius.*

Why?

Why would anyone want to suppress genius? Well, it is not intentional. It is not a plot. Genius is an innocent casualty in society's efforts to train children away from natural-born foolishness.

There is a Fool in each of us, you know.
A rash, brash, harebrained, audacious, imprudent,
Ill-suited, spontaneous, impolitic, daredevil Fool, which,
In most of us,
Was long ago hog-tied and locked in the basement.
If you want to see a full-fledged Fool in action,
Watch an undisciplined child.
(The more undisciplined, the better!)
Oblivious to concepts of appropriate behavior,
Driven by rampant curiosity and innocent lust.
Raw genius,
Resolutely stumbling into hurt and wondrous discovery.
Inspired, annoying,
Rapturous, petulant.
The creative savage of our being.

Savages, Fools,
Do not a society make.
So we tame the little Yahoos.
We teach them the meaning of the word "no."
We teach them the benefits of boundaries.
We teach them the value of our learned lessons.
When our teachings fall short,
Our society begins to unravel,
And the quality of our culture declines.
So tame, we must.
But we have been slow to learn how to tame the Fool
Without also interring
The Fool's innate creativity and inborn genius.

With the bath water, the baby is cast out.

The Diamond Cartel, which exists to keep as many diamonds underground as is necessary to maintain the market value of diamonds aboveground at an artificially high level, operates with as low a profile as it possibly can. It wishes it could be invisible, but, alas, its existence is known.

But! There is at least one invisible cartel: the Genius Cartel.

Shall we expose it?

To endure, a society needs a vision of what it means to be normal:

> nọr′măl, a. [L. *normalis, norma,* a carpenter's rule] 1: of or conforming to the accepted model, pattern or standard. 2: not abnormal.

But creativity and genius have not so much to do with being normal as with being original:

> ô-rig′i-năl, a. [L. *originalis, origo,* origin or beginning] 1: having to do with an origin, source or beginning. 2: never having existed before. 3: created or invented independent of already existing ideas or works.

Our creative genius is the fountainhead of originality. It fires our compulsion to evolve. It inspires us to challenge norms. Creative genius is about flying to new heights on untested wings. It is about the danger of crashing. It is amorphous, magical, unmeasurable and unpredictable.

Threatened by all of this, society appoints its clandestine cartel to put a cap on imaginative brilliance.

As old as civilization, the Genius Cartel is an originality-suppression agency that permeates our lives. It tyrannized Galileo into recanting the fruits of his own scientific genius. It handed Socrates a cup of hemlock, put a match to Joan of Arc, and fomented the crucifixion of Christ.

Among its collaborators, the cartel numbers lawmakers, lawkeepers, bureaucrats, clergy, teachers, parents, siblings, husbands, wives, lovers, co-workers, bosses, friends, acquaintances and total strangers. Anyone who, having surrendered to the status quo, has become averse to change.

From cradle to grave, the pressure is on: **BE NORMAL**

Those who somehow side-step that pressure and let their genius show are customarily ridiculed, reviled or otherwise discountenanced.

Small wonder that by sixth grade, hardly anyone will admit to creative genius.

But we need our genius to bail ourselves out of the messes we continually get ourselves into. So, individually, we must override the cartel, set aside our herd longing for security through sameness and seek the help of our natural genius. Yours and mine.

Having trouble with the idea of your own genius? My guess is that there was a time — perhaps when you were very young — when you had at least a fleeting notion of your own genius and were just waiting for some authority figure to come along and validate it for you.

But none ever came.

Of course not. It is not the business of authority figures to validate genius, because genius threatens authority.

But there is still hope. You are an adult now. As an adult, you can choose to become your own authority figure. As such, you will be in a position to redeem the creative genius in you that was put to sleep when the Fool was being tamed.

Reviving the creative genius in you is the beginning of Orbit.

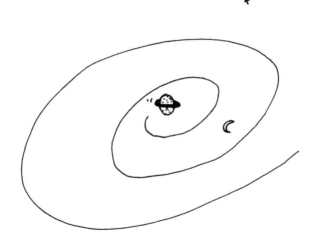

Chapter Two

THE GIANT HAIRBALL

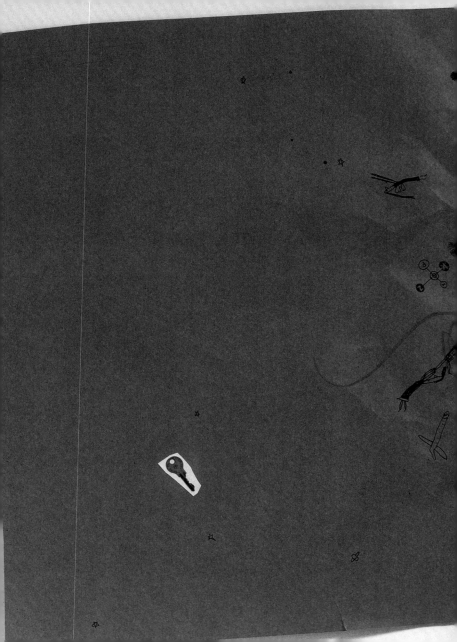

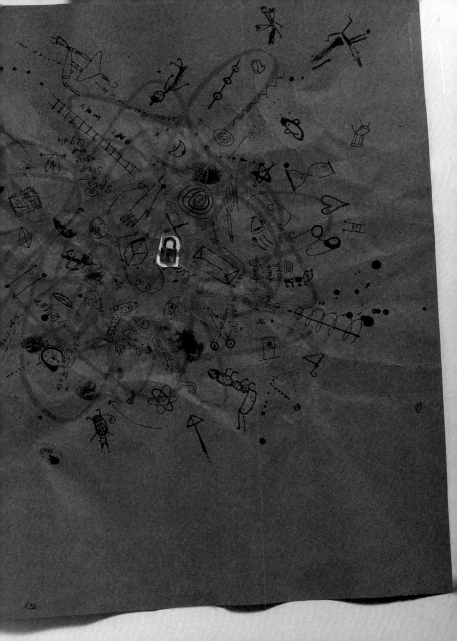

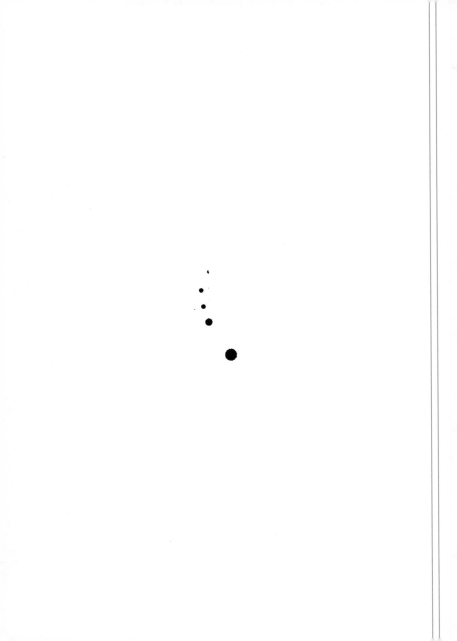

"This is a giant hairball."

So spoke George Parker in a meeting of his department heads and senior managers. George was an advertising man who had left N.W. Ayer in Chicago and come to Kansas City to play a roaring Peter the Great to the Creative division of Hallmark Cards for a decade before moving on. The crude little *hairball* comment was in reference to his very own Creative division.

"What a disgusting term!" I thought. (A certain roughneck flamboyance was a part of Mr. Parker's carefully groomed style.) I rejected the image. Put it out of my head. But the metaphor was not to be dismissed so easily. A couple of weeks later, I was driving down the street, my mind in neutral, when, quite suddenly, a thought popped up:

> *"Wait a minute! There's a time when there is no hairball. So where do hairballs come from?"*

I pondered a moment then reasoned:

> *"Well, two hairs unite. Then they're joined by another. And another. And another. Before long, where there was once nothing, this tangled, impenetrable mass has begun to form."*

George's words were finally getting through to me:

> *"The Creative Division <u>is</u> a giant hairball,"* I thought. *"More than that... <u>Hallmark's</u> a giant hairball!"*

HALLMARK THE HAIRBALL

As the story goes: On January 9, 1910, 18-year-old Joyce Clyde Hall boarded a train in Norfolk, Nebraska, with a one-way ticket to Kansas City, Missouri. Upon arriving at the old Union Station, Hall made his way to the local YMCA, checked in and set about to establish a mail-order postcard business. It is said that he stored his entire, initial inventory under the bed in his 12-foot-by-12-foot room at the "Y" — a modest beginning for an enterprise that would give birth to Hallmark Cards, the largest social expression company in the world.

There was no greeting card industry to speak of way back then so there were few precedents for young Hall's fledgling enterprise. With scant trade precedents, he had to base many of his decisions on common sense, intuition and creative instinct. Original thinking would have been mandatory. He may very well have said to himself something like:

> *"My gut tells me it would be most effective if I did this this way. And it would make sense to do that that way."*

This and *that*, Hall's first two business decisions, were also the first two hairs of the hairball that was to become Hallmark. For decades, J.C. Hall and the thousands of Hallmarkers who have followed him have — quite appropriately — been making business decision after business decision, creating procedures and generating policies. And in so doing, they have been adding countless hairs to the Hairball. Intricate patterns of effective behavior have grown around the lessons of success and failure, creating a Gordian knot of Corporate Normalcy (i.e., conformity with the *"accepted model, pattern or standard"* of the corporate mind set).

This Corporate Normalcy is Hallmark's success formula. This is the essence of Hallmark. And the Hairball of Hallmark.

Every new policy is another hair for the Hairball. Hairs are never taken away, only added. Even frequent reorganizations have failed to remove hairs (people, sometimes; hairs, never). Quite the contrary, each reorganization seems to add a *whole new layer* of hairs. The Hairball grows enormous.

With the increase in the Hairball's mass comes a corresponding increase in the Hairball's gravity. There is such a thing as Corporate Gravity. As in the world of physics, so too in the corporate world: *The gravitational pull a body exerts increases as the mass of that body increases.* And, like physical gravity, it is the nature of Corporate Gravity to suck everything into the mass — in this case, into the mass of Corporate Normalcy.

The trouble with this is that Corporate Normalcy derives from and is dedicated to past realities and past successes. There is no room in the Hairball of Corporate Normalcy for original thinking or primary creativity. Resynthesizing *past* successes is the habit of the Hairball. *Tick*

Tock

I worked at Hallmark for 30 years. To the day.

Like the many other artists and writers on the payroll — Hallmark likes to boast that it has the largest creative staff in the world, which has sometimes numbered as high as 600 — my role, my assignment, was to *create* for the company.

> çrē·āte', *v. t.*; created, *pt. pp.*; creating, ppr, [L. *creatus, creare*, to create, make] 1: to bring into existence; cause to be; originate. 2: to give new character, function or interpretation to. 3: to cause; produce.

So create I did. But during those 30 years, there was not a day when I was not subject to the inexorable pull of Corporate Gravity tug, tug, tugging me toward (and, during one unhappy year, right into) the tangle of the Hairball, where the ghosts of past successes outvote original thinking.

To tap the ability to create, you must spiritually soar into the thin air of the stratosphere — blue sky — where it is possible *"to bring into existence"* from nothing an original concept. Hairballs detest thin air like nature abhors a vacuum. A concrete world where precedents take precedence is a reality more to a Hairball's liking. A world honey-combed with the established guidelines, techniques, methodologies, systems and equations that are the heart of a Hairball's gravity.

Many a Hallmarker succumb to the pull of this relentless gravity. They are the ones who, suspended in the grey sameness of the bowels of the institution, wonder:

"What year is it?"
(So much for the energy of *their* careers.)

Others, in their attempts to avoid the threatened limbo of the Hairball, escape to other endeavors — often, ironically, to other Hairballs.

Then there are those few (some still there, I hear) who manage to actively engage the opportunities Hallmark presents without being sucked into the Hairball of Hallmark. This is accomplished by *Orbiting*.

✿

Orbiting is responsible creativity: vigorously exploring and operating beyond the Hairball of the corporate mind set, beyond *"accepted models, patterns, or standards"* — all the while remaining connected to the spirit of the corporate mission.

To find Orbit around a corporate Hairball is to find a place of balance where you benefit from the physical, intellectual and philosophical resources of the organization without becoming entombed in the bureaucracy of the institution.

If you are interested (and it is not for everyone), you can achieve Orbit by finding the personal courage to be genuine and to take the best course of action to get the job done rather than following the pallid path of corporate appropriateness.

To be of optimum value to the corporate endeavor, you must invest enough individuality to counteract the pull of Corporate Gravity, but not so much that you escape that pull altogether. Just enough to stay out of the Hairball.

Through this measured assertion of your own uniqueness, it is possible to establish a dynamic relationship with the Hairball — to Orbit around the institutional mass. If you do this, you make an asset of the gravity in that it becomes a force that keeps you from flying out into the overwhelming nothingness of deep space.

But if you allow that same gravity to suck you into the bureaucratic Hairball, you will find yourself in a different kind of nothingness. The nothingness of a normalcy made stagnant by a compulsion to cling to past successes. The nothingness of the Hairball.

BEAUTY Delight Pure Paradox

Chapter Three

PINK BUDDHA

When I first joined Hallmark, I neither knew nor cared about Hairballs. I'd been hired by the Editorial department to be one of two sketch artists working to serve a whole staff of writers and editors. I liked that. Much better than being one of the scores of artists milling around in the Design department, which was right next door to us. But I did not like the deference to conformity that I found in *all* the departments I came in contact with. After having worked for a couple of daily newspapers where a measure of eccentricity was celebrated, the spirit of this world of corporate decorum, new to me, seemed incongruously anemic compared to the colorful, exciting products we were working on. I was beginning to regret that I had even hired on at "the Big Grey Place," as the corporation was referred to by some of the less reverent old-timers.

Then I started hearing stories. Wonderful stories. About kinky artists, oddball writers and bizarre behavior in a department that was sequestered from the mainstream: Contemporary Design, Hallmark's crazy aunt in the west wing. The scuttlebutt was that this department was started back in the 1950s while J.C. Hall was away from the company for an extended period. When Mr. Hall returned, although he disliked (some say hated) Contemporary Design's products, he saw that they were selling extremely well. So they were, obviously, meeting heretofore untapped desires of the buying public — not to mention adding to the health of Hallmark's bottom line. Being a sensible businessman, "The Old Man" allowed Contemporary to continue. But from the beginning, its status was that of a stepchild — an unruly, but prodigiously productive stepchild.

I wanted to work there. However, it was a small group, and a lot of other artists and writers wanted to work there, too. It took me two-and-a-half years to finagle my way in.

Contemporary was everything I had heard and hoped. More, even. There was a kind of a kindergarten chaos from which W. Robert McCloskey, the department director, orchestrated a sparkling flow of saleable product. I was in awe of Mr. McCloskey, as he was addressed with unintentional reverence by his unwitting followers. (Addressed as Mr. McCloskey, but referred to as "Big Pink" — because of his imposing physique and rubicund complexion.) In the guise of an administrator, he lavished *invisible leadership* on a crew of zanies who would have spurned overt authority in a minute. A superb diplomat who kept the predators of the Big Grey Place at bay, McCloskey presided over a Mad Hatter's tea party with a wily sense of mission and an enduring, customer-oriented vision.

I would not have described it with these words back then, but this was my introduction to Hairballs and Orbiting. Here was Hallmark the Hairball barreling along with all the success-fired momentum of its own cultural imperatives (compulsions). And, Orbiting around it — responsible to, but not controlled by, the Hairball — was Contemporary Design. There was a beautiful balance in this Orbiting. McCloskey was determined to run his own show. But he knew that to stay in business, he had to satisfy the ambitions and honor the ideals of J.C. Hall and Hallmark proper. Fortunately, McCloskey's ideals harmonized with Hallmark's, but his passion for creating greeting cards that were countercultural in tone lay outside Mr. Hall's comfort zone. To ease Hall's discomfort, McCloskey labored mightily to produce a line that was continually and exceptionally profitable. And he spent countless hours lobbying Hall and his courtiers on the value and values of Contemporary's then-renegade product line.

Of course, to create a renegade product line would require renegade artists and writers. McCloskey recruited them with gleeful genius.

Renegades are tricky people to deal with. By definition, they resist being led. McCloskey's response was to draw on his uncanny talent for leading-without-leading. He understood that renegades go off on tangents; that was just fine with him. Flying off on a tangent is the first step in the process of going into Orbit. That fit right in with his plans. He realized, although I think he would not have used these terms, that Contemporary's success would eventually make it a Hairball, too — a much smaller Hairball than Hallmark, but a Hairball nevertheless. Hairball is policy, procedure, conformity, compliance, rigidity and submission to status quo, while Orbiting is originality, rules-breaking, non-conformity, experimentation, and innovation. To keep his department young and yeasty, McCloskey wanted his crew, at least those of us who were eager and willing to make the trip, to be in Orbits of our own. In Orbit, where invention happens. So he would let us fly off on our tangents. But, so that we would not go spinning into deep space, where we would be useless to him and to Hallmark, he would, with his own unique brand of gravitational pull, transform our tangents into *Orbits*, allowing us to travel paths related to the system... but not of the system.

How would he do this — exert this gravitational pull? More than any other way, through storytelling. A master raconteur, he was never without an anecdote about this or that. Like some jolly, inscrutable, business buddha, he would reach out with the subtle power of an entertaining parable or puzzling corporate koan and gently, but resolutely, nudge us into Orbits. Always entertaining, always elegantly germane, always with his own master plan in mind. McCloskey, artist and merchant (he had graduated from the Rhode Island School of Design and then worked in his family's department store), offered us — ever so graciously — his remarkable range of hard-earned insights into the practical art of creating fresh, tasteful products that would appeal to a broad audience.

After I'd put in a couple of productive years in the department, McCloskey promoted me to design supervisor. And guess what? *I* became a little Hairball — just like my fellow supervisors. And, in the best instances, artists and writers orbited around us.

Picture in your mind the complex movement in all of these writers and artists traveling in tangents-become-Orbits around little supervisor Hairballs. The supervisors, in turn, Orbited Mr. McCloskey's larger Contemporary Hairball. And it was similarly in Orbit around the giant Hallmark Hairball. A never-changing...

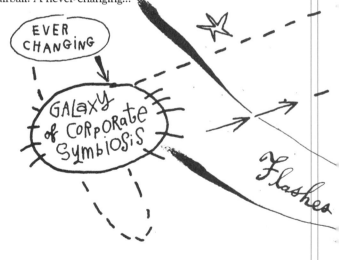

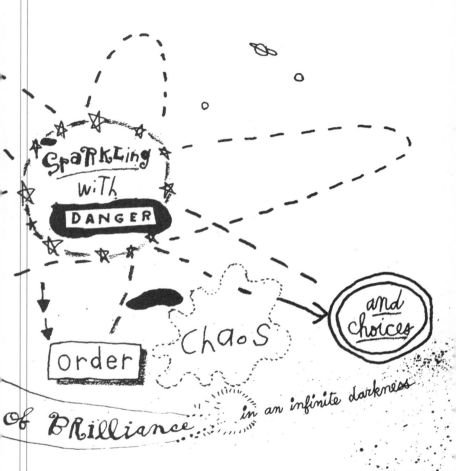

SpaRKLing
with
DANGER

order

Chaos

and choices

of BRilliance ... in an infinite darkness

A NEVER-ENDING EMPTINESS
FILLED WITH OPPORTUNITIES
TO BECOME LOST AND TO GROW

41

Chapter Four

PREPARING FOR LIFT-OFF

You can Orbit too soon, and it can turn out badly. So it is important to grow into readiness. And you can do just that *in* the Hairball. Its tangledness can serve as protection, a briar patch — a cocoon in which to prepare for the challenges of Orbit.

A word of caution, though: Cocoons can be paralyzing.

Being infinite, the whole of reality is too much for the conscious human mind to grasp. The best any one of us can do is to take the biggest slice of Infinite Reality that we can hold — intellectually, spiritually and emotionally — and make that slice our personal sense of what is real. But no matter how broad it is, any human perception of reality can be no more than a tiny sliver of Infinite Reality.

Civilization also has a limited perception of Infinite Reality. And with a haughty self-assurance, it imposes that perception on us until we think it is our own. The same is true of the companies we work for. They have their perceptions of reality and they impose them on us. As a result, we are wrapped in a cocoon of realities perceived by others who came before us. It is a cocoon that gives us a sense of emotional security through connection to a shared belief. But it is also a shroud that binds and cripples us as surely as the ancient social abuse of binding Chinese women's feet crippled them.

Incongruous as it may be, I have always both accepted and rejected the social order's view of what is appropriate. I hunger for the comfort that can come from devotion to herd wisdom. Yet, at the same time, I remain desperate to flee the soul-wilting thatch of society's rules and standards and fly to the more uncertain but broader possibilities of living originally.

45.

Lucky for me, Hallmark proved to be a cocoon where I could indulge both of these conflicting drives. I was able to spend most of my career drawing and writing funny, anti-establishment greeting cards, venting my rage against society's restrictions in a way that filled me with mischievous exhilaration, made a profit for the company and thus, brought me material security. It seemed a livable compromise.

Eventually, however, annual salary increases pulled me out of that niche and pushed me toward middle management. It was an unwelcome fate for an aspiring Orbiter, but one I was, over the course of time, able to elude by becoming, instead, a self-appointed mentor. That, in turn, led me into an uncertain but passionate quest to free human spirits, both others and my own. I gave up sniping at the power of the social order and, instead, focused on becoming a champion of autonomy. With a thrilling sense of mission, I contrived a private agenda to subvert the stupefying power of the corporate culture and provoke the emancipation of creative genius. My mission became my career. And while I continued to work on specific product or marketing-related projects, my passion turned toward something deeper. Bob Kipp, my last boss at Hallmark, described it to a magazine writer:

> *"Gordon's job... is to keep track of new ideas and sort of sense the spiritual needs of the organization and address them."*

To address those spiritual needs, I borrowed from the techniques and vocabulary of psychotherapy. I threw in some jargon ("Cocoons" and "Hairballs" and "Tangents" and "Orbits") and realities of my own. I also concocted catalytic rituals and psychic exercises — anything that might catch the attention of the sleepwalking geniuses and lure them to wakefulness, help them find the courage to be who they truly were instead of who they thought the company expected them to be and entice them into meeting life with an exuberance that befits humanity.

Some came to describe me as *"the bridge between Hallmark's creative forces and its executives."* Others saw me as con man, charlatan. There was some truth in both assessments, I would guess. But beyond that, by serving the vocation that issued from my instincts, I emerged from the Company Cocoon. Slipped the bonds of the Hairball of Corporate Normalcy. Ascended into Orbit.

> *"... if you do follow your bliss, you put yourself on a kind*
> *of track that has been there all the while, waiting for you,*
> *and the life you ought to be living is the one you are living."*

Joseph Campbell, *The Power of Myth*

Orbiting is following your bliss.

A CHICKEN'S FATE

My father spent the summer of 1904 on the farm of an aunt and uncle who lived a stone's throw northeast of Lucknow in Bruce County, Ontario, Canada.

It so happened that the aunt and uncle had a son the same age as my father. Story has it that when the two boys were together, they were a couple of hellers with a genius for mischief.

One sunny Sunday, the boys feigned stomachaches and so were excused from going to church. Uncle hitched the horse to the family's carriage and helped his wife on board, and the two of them rode off to town for their communal worship. Of course, as soon as their carriage was out of sight around the bend, the boys' stomachaches miraculously disappeared, and the two 10-year-olds set about to find something to do.

Wanting to impress my father, a city boy, the cousin asked:

"Do you know how to mesmerize a chicken?"

"Mesmerize? Uh-uh. What's that?"

"Follow me."

The cousin led the way to a ramshackle chicken coop out behind the farmhouse. There he selected a fine white hen. He carried her under his arm to the front of the house, produced a piece of chalk and drew a short line on the porch. He stood the creature over the chalk line and held her beak to it. After a moment or so, the boy slowly removed his hands. The chicken stood motionless, beak to the chalk line, hypnotized. My father hooted with glee.

"Let's do another one! Let's do another one!" he pleaded.

The two boys ran back to the hen house for another chicken. And another. And another. Before long, the hen house was empty, and the front porch was filled with 70 or so dead-silent, stark-still chickens straddling chalk lines, beaks seemingly glued to the porch.

The boys, too, seemed hypnotized — mesmerized by this glorious example of their own cleverness. A breeze gently rippled the feathery coats of the unmoving chickens. In the distance, soft thudding hooves and the rattle of turning carriage wheels signaled the return of Aunt and Uncle. Wouldn't they be surprised at this latest joke? (Aunt and Uncle did take a perverse pride in the boys' escapades.)

But wait! There were two carriages, not one. Behind the family's carriage followed a small runabout driven by the preacher! Aunt and Uncle had invited their Scottish Presbyterian reverend to come to lunch (or dinner, as they said back there, back then). Worse, Aunt had already explained to the preacher that boys had not been at church because they were ill.

Upon seeing the fowl foolery, Uncle flew into an embarrassed rage, leapt off the carriage and bounded onto the porch, place-kicking chicken after chicken back to consciousness. Feathers and clucking and curses filled the air. The preacher, scandalized, turned his carriage around and, without a word, fled back to town, never to return.

The same thing that happened to those chickens can happen to you. When you join an organization, you are, without fail, taken by the back of the neck and pushed down and down until your beak is on a line — not a chalk line, but a company line. And the company line says things like:

> "This is our history. This is our philosophy. These are our policies. These are our procedures. These are our politics. This is simply the way we are."

If you are not careful, you will be hypnotized by this line.

And what a pity if that happens.

When you come into an organization, you bring with you an arcane potency, which stems, in part, from your uniqueness. That, in turn, is rooted in a complex mosaic of personal history that is original, unfathomable, inimitable. There has never been anyone quite like you, and there never will be. Consequently, you can contribute something to an endeavor that nobody else can. There is a power in your uniqueness — an inexplicable, unmeasurable power... *a magic.*

But if you are hypnotized by an organization's culture, you become separated from your personal magic and cannot tap it to help achieve the goals of the organization. In losing connection with your one-of-a-kind magic, you are reduced to nothing more than part of the headcount. Deep inside the Hairball.

So, whenever you feel your head being pushed down onto an organization's cultural chalk line, remember the challenge is to move out of the way, to choose not to be mesmerized by the culture of the company. Instead, find the goals of the organization that touch your heart and release your passion to follow those goals.

It is a delicate balance, resisting the hypnotic spell of an organization's culture and, at the same time, remaining committed from the heart to the personally relevant goals of the organization. But if you can achieve that balance and maintain it, you will be out of the Hairball and into Orbit, the only place where you can tap your one-of-a-kind magic, your genius, your limitless creativity.

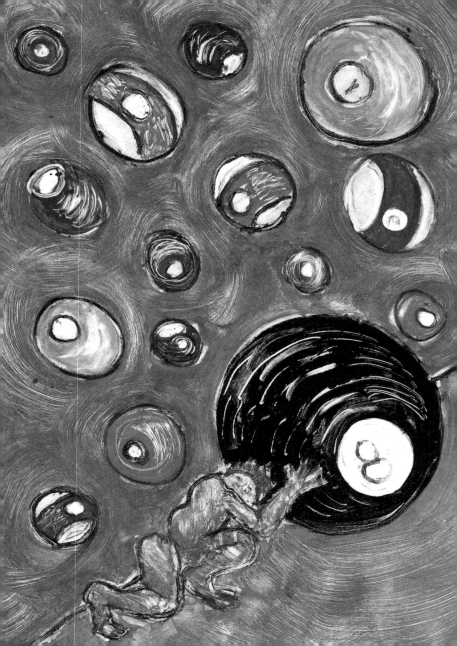

THOU SHALT NOT HAVE IT EASY

In June 1989, I was engaged to speak at a conference held for a special project group at one of the computer giants in Northern California. School teachers participating in the project had been brought together from around the country to reconnect with their mentors at the corporation's headquarters. Although the gathering was to last a week, I was to be there only the first day. In the afternoon I would offer my presentation and workshop. In the morning, I was merely an observing guest.

Things began on a traditional note. A woman who had been key in organizing the whole affair stood before the assembled group to offer a welcome. In her opening remarks, she thanked those who had so generously helped put the conference together, adding:

"You gave so much; you really made my job easy."

To my surprise, the response to this acknowledgement was an immediate outburst of heckling.

The woman's face flushed, and although she kept smiling, her words betrayed a sudden defensiveness. I found myself wondering if, maybe, it was not okay at this company to have an easy job. My suspicion was confirmed later in the morning when another hapless soul let it slip that a recently assigned project had been smooth sailing all the way. Again the teasing erupted, convincing me that having an easy job was taboo in this corporation's culture.

At our lunch break, I excused myself and rushed up to my hotel room. There, I sketched an eight ball to add to a series of drawings that were to be a part of my afternoon presentation. Later, during the presentation, when someone asked about the eight ball, I told the group that the drawing was intended to remind me of the suspicion

that had stirred in me that morning, a suspicion that had brought to mind the time my father gave me a lesson in the game of pool.

During the course of his singularly unsuccessful efforts to make a pool player out of me, my father told me that when he was a young man, he had been a fanatic about the game. He told me of learning, during that time, of a championship match that was to be held in the city where he then lived, Edmonton, Alberta. My father reminisced over the excitement he had felt as he entered the exhibition hall and scrambled through the milling crowd to find his seat. He spoke of his surge of anticipation when the house lights dimmed. In the center of the hall, an ornately carved pool table stood in a rectangle of brilliant light. A short, stout figure in black tuxedo emerged from the darkness and stood a moment, contemplating the precise triangle of colored pool balls waiting at the table's end. With unhurried deliberation, the man removed his coat, folded it and set it aside. From the darkness, he drew a pool cue and, eyes fixed on the table, chalked the cue's tip, repositioned the white cue ball and silently bent over his cue. Taking aim... CRACK!... he sent the colored balls scattering like little bumper cars across the green felt arena. The match had begun.

"*Two ball.*" Click... thunk.

"*Seven ball.*" Click... thunk.

"*Four ball.*" Click... thunk.

One after another, the man dispatched the balls to their pockets, and the match turned out to be no match at all. My father recalled his mounting disappointment as he watched the champion make one "easy" shot after another. Expecting to be thrilled by daring and spectacular competition, my father was, instead, treated to an evening of quiet mastery.

I suggested to my new friends at the computer company that they might consider making room in their minds for the possibility that, sometimes, when they see a colleague whose job seems easy, they may in fact be witnessing a champion at play.

When a corporation prizes those who are heroically overworked in stress-filled jobs, a siren song whispers to everyone else in the organization:

> *Make your job difficult,*
> *stretch yourself thin,*
> *stress yourself out*
> *and eventually you, too,*
>
> *may be honored with executive approval.*

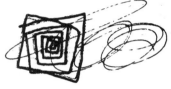

> *If you desire the blessing of the Mighty Corporate Fathers:*
> > *work longer hours (than is sensible);*
> > *take on more responsibility (than is sensible);*
> > *make your job harder (than is sensible).*

> *Do this, and your sacrifices will be celebrated*
> *and your worth confirmed.*

This cultural seduction plays into the old illusion that if we just work hard enough, and if we just work long enough...

> we will finally be found valuable...
> finally be found loveable...
> and finally find security.

Instead, what the seduction delivers — if we buy into it — is a workplace where the quality of life is continually eroded by contrived travail.

Wouldn't a more promising choice be
to turn your back
on the
Overwork-as-an-end-in-itself Game

And, instead,
enlist the hidden genius within you
and develop the skills
to play like a champion?

Chapter Seven

WHAT YOU DON'T SEE IS WHAT YOU GET

In the upper reaches of the hierarchy at Hallmark Cards, there was a Prince of Profit whose forté was control. And although I suspect control was only a part of his responsibilities, it often seemed to be the primary focus of his passion. His more-than-firm hand on the reins enhanced an already enviable bottom line. And because Hallmark has such a generous profit-sharing program, I was a beneficiary of his effectiveness and fully appreciated his efforts on my behalf. However, I did have one problem with him: He did not seem to appreciate the phenomenon of creativity.

It was my problem, not his, and so I generated a fantasy in the hope of working through my problem. I would like, if I may, to share that fantasy with you:

> **Picture in your mind's eye a pastureland of gently rolling hills painted in the rich greens of early spring. Within the meandering confines of a zigzag, split-rail fence stands a scattered herd of black-and-white holstein dairy cows. The sun is shining, and some of the cows have sought the cool protection of the field's occasional massive shade trees. Others are clustered idly around a large, sun-sparkling pond. Most are quietly eating grass. One regurgitates her cud and chews it.**

> **Outside the zigzag of the fence stands a rotund gentleman in a $700, power-blue, pinstripe suit. He is leaning over the fence — as best he can. One hand is holding his unbuttoned jacket against his generous belly so that the suit's fine cloth will not be soiled by the fence's grimy rails. His other hand is shaking a stern finger at the cows. He shouts:**

> ***"You slackers get to work, or I'll have you butchered!"***

63.

What this man does not understand is that, even as he threatens them, the cows are performing the miracle of turning grass into milk. Nor does he understand that his shouting will not cause the cows to produce more milk.

If we drew a line to represent a creative occurrence…

… the only portion that would reflect measurable productivity would be a short segment at the end of the line:

measurable evidence of creativity

This line segment is the equivalent of the cow's time in the barn, hooked up to the milking machine. This is when productivity is tangible, measurable. But the earlier, larger part of the event, when the milk was actually being created, remains invisible.

invisible creative activity

The invisible portion is equivalent to the time the cow spends out in the pasture, seemingly idle, but, in fact, performing the alchemy of transforming grass into milk.

A management obsessed with productivity usually has little patience for the quiet time essential to profound creativity. Its dream of dreams is to put the cows on the milking machine 24 hours a day. Crazy? It is happening in workplaces all over the country: workers being sucked inside-out by corporate milking machines.

Welcome to the
*If-we-work-hard-enough-long-enough-burn-ourselves-
out-enough-we'll-succeed-through-control* Hairball.

And while, as Thomas Edison said...

"Genius is 10 percent inspiration and 90 percent perspiration"

... too many enterprises seem self-destructively locked into a
debilitating reality of 100 percent perspiration and zero percent
inspiration.

A healthier alternative is the Orbit of trust that allows time —
without immediate, concrete evidence of productivity — for the
miracle of creativity to occur.

N O   A C C E S S

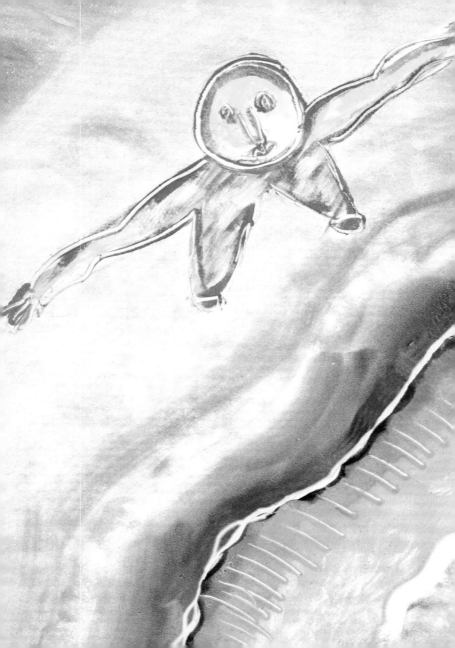

The rim of the cliffs that tower over Blacks Beach in La Jolla is a favorite launching pad for San Diego hang gliders.

I had just finished a presentation to a conference of the American Gas Association at the Sheraton Grande Torre Pines. Now, free for the afternoon, I strolled over to those cliffs in a swimsuit, T-shirt and scruffy sneakers to watch the adventurers-who-would-be-birds make their leaps of faith out over the Pacific Ocean. It was a sight that inspired awe.

(For about two minutes.)

Fascinating as these graceful gliders were, my eyes soon tired of squinting into the brilliant California sky, and my interest waned. It was time to move on to my next whim, a swim in the surf.

Heading toward the cliff's edge, in search of a way down to the beach, I was stopped by a line of posts driven into the ground six feet apart, connected by a steel chain loosely threaded through a hole drilled in the top of each post. Various large signs established the seriousness of the barrier's purpose:

71.

Curious about just how dangerous the cliffs really were, I stepped over the chain at the lowest point of its sweep, midway between posts, and walked over to the brink to have a look. Two hundred feet below me lay the beach. Faint sounds of laughter beckoned me to join the small clusters of people playing in the sand at the ocean's surging edge.

"They got down there," I thought. *"I should be able to."*

I scanned the face of the cliff. Safe descent seemed reasonably achievable. In a giddy sense of adventure, inspired perhaps by the daring of the hang gliders I had admired just minutes before, I began the climb down.

Interesting substance that cliff is made of. It seemed to me a sort of sunbaked mixture of sand and clay, substantial in appearance, but not in fact. My weight on a firm-appearing foothold caused the foothold simply to crumble and give way.

That added to the excitement.

I experienced a subtle sense of relief as I climbed below the line-of-sight of the clifftop. Now I felt shielded from possible disapproving stares of the less adventurous who, I fantasized, were so easily daunted by the signs' warnings. The descent had begun well and, as I scrambled from one crumbling foothold down to the next, I found myself basking in a growing self-congratulation over choosing not to be limited by the prohibitions of some unknown authority.

Thirty feet into the climb, I came to a place where further descent would require that I execute what I might euphemistically call a controlled slide down to a broad ledge 15 feet below. There was no doubt in my mind that the ledge would hold me. There was also no doubt that, should I decide to make this maneuver, there would be no way to climb back up. Clearly, this was a point of no return.

I slid.

It was exhilarating. And the ledge did catch me — another little triumph.

The climbing became easy now, but with fewer and fewer alternative courses as I moved further down the face of the precipice. Eventually, my choices of route led me to a long, V-shaped trough that angled steeply toward the beach — at this point, I would guess, 70 or 80 feet beneath me. Facing out to sea, I wedged myself into the trough and slowly ratcheted my body downward until I reached the edge of a drop-off. Even leaning forward as far as I dared — just this side of losing my balance and plummeting to the beach — I could not strain forward far enough to see how big a drop awaited me.

What to do? I sat a minute and then decided to take my chances with the unknown. Ever so slowly, I began to ease myself over the edge. Paused. Thought better of it. And wiggled back into the relative safety of the trough.

I was sitting still now. My mind began to shut down. I heard the off-shore breeze, not noticed before, whispering to me of my aloneness. Arms and legs spread-eagled, clinging to the cliff in my tragi-comic self-crucifixion, I gazed longingly at the casual communion of the bathers below me, noticing for the first time that they were naked. (It turns out that Blacks Beach is a nudist beach.) Laughter drifted up. Time passed. A certain peace settled over me. I suppose I was waiting.

One of three men puttering about in the dry sand above the high-tide mark happened to look up and spy me on my unlikely perch. We locked gazes in a freeze-frame of uncertainty. As people will, others on the beach noticed my discoverer's curiosity and looked up. A small crowd gathered — necks craning, eyes squinting, hands held to brows as eyeshades. I resisted a bizarre urge to bless my naked flock with an unauthorized sign of the cross. It would have been a confusing signal.

My discoverer called to me. I could not hear. He climbed carefully up the cliff as far as he safely could and called again. This time I heard:

"Did you fall off a hang glider?"

(This would have been the only legitimate reason for my being where I was.)

"No."

"Are you injured?"

"No."

"What are you doing there?"

"I'm stuck."

(I almost choked on the words.)

"Don't move. Do not move. I'll go and get help."

He climbed back down and trotted away. To my relief, the crowd of onlookers soon lost interest in me and dispersed. In the solitude of my fool's perch, I pondered my prospects. I winced at the possibility that I might become an unwilling star on *Rescue 911*. I prayed that the day would be filled with noteworthy national and international events so there would not be room on the evening news for the story of my misadventure.

My discoverer returned:

"They'll be here in about 20 minutes," he shouted reassuringly.

I thanked him, and he rejoined his buddies on the beach. Twenty minutes. I checked my watch.

"That's too long," I thought. The muscles in my left thigh were already trembling from fatigue.

"I'm not going to be able to hang on that long. I'll slide over the edge before they even get here." (Now I was nearing a second edge, that of panic.)

The folks at the Gas Association had given me, as a memento of their conference, a desk clock. Tastefully set in a small, wedge-shaped block of rosewood, trimmed with a brass rim, the clock's face carries Roman numerals. Beneath the face, a small plaque, brass also, is inscribed: AGA. I thought of the clock now. I remembered it lying on the bed where I had casually tossed it, back in my hotel room where the drapes were drawn, and the air conditioning was on, and it was safe. I envied that clock. Closing my eyes, I pictured the clock, pictured the Roman numerals. Roman numerals seem so permanent. I pictured the sweep second hand moving with a soundless grace past the Roman numerals... around and around and around and around...

I opened my eyes with a start, squinting at the brightness of the day. A helicopter was coming along the coast from the south. I looked at my watch. Forty minutes! I had spent 40 minutes in the calming refuge of my visualization. Now the image of the clock was pushed aside by a rush of relief and anxiety — relief that I was about to be rescued, anxiety that I was about to catch hell from the authorities. (I have an enduring fear of authority). The helicopter's arrival seemed a mixed blessing.

What arrival? The helicopter flew right past. Missed me completely.

"Damn!"

Down on the beach, my loyal discoverer stood watching the helicopter grow smaller and smaller up the coast. Turning deliberately, he searched the shoreline for a stick and lettered with it large in the sand that had been made smooth by the tide's coming in and going out:

and drew an arrow pointing toward me.

The helicopter, a speck in the distance now, started, finally, to grow larger again. Would it miss me a second time? No. The sign in the sand did its work. The helicopter stopped above it, directly opposite me. Large, blue capital letters on the white fuselage proclaimed:

SHERIFF

Because the tinted glass of the cockpit hid from view whatever crew was on board, I was drawn to invest the helicopter with a personality. For the moment, it became the ultimate authority figure, reminiscent of my grade school principal: judging, menacing, inscrutable. Emotionally, I regressed to age six.

The machine moved toward me. To pluck me from my predicament? No such luck. The rotors' wild turbulence whipped up a blinding maelstrom of dust and sand. The machine backed off, hovered for a moment, watching me, then flew away. The stillness that followed was a balm that faded to a numbing sense of isolation and helplessness. All I could do was wait. It was not so long a wait this time. Within five minutes of the helicopter's leaving, a king-cab pickup truck ladened

with rescue equipment came churning down the beach and swerved to a halt beneath my fool's roost. Four lifeguards piled out, all serious and full of energy. They surveyed, conferred, assessed and, apparently, decided. One climbed half way up to me:

> "We'll have to come down from above."

> "Okay."

(Was I giving my consent?)

Ten minutes later, sporadic showers of sand and crumbled clay cascaded over and around me. In the position I was in, I found it impossible to look up. But a quiet grunting and the clicking sounds of climbing-gear-in-use told me I was about to meet my rescuer... and reprimander.

> "Hi, my name's Bruce." The friendliness of the voice above me came as a surprise. "What's your name?"

> "Gordon," I replied.

> "Well, Gordon, I want you to sit very still. Don't move. I'm going to come right over top of you, so it's important that you not move."

> "I understand."

There were sounds of Bruce jockeying into position, then another grunt and a swoosh as he kicked away from the cliff. Then — presto! — his hulk appeared in front of me, blocking out the sun. His sturdy hiking boots were firmly planted one on each side of my feet. Ropes and clasps and hooks that inspired trust girdled his sweat-soaked bathing suit. Two lines — one taut, the other slack — stretched to some secure support on the cliff top above.

"I've got him, and he appears to be OK," Bruce reported into a small radio transmitter strapped to his right shoulder. *"Are you?"* He looked me in the eye. I found comfort in his reassuring, even friendly, smile.

"Yes. Thank you."

Explaining each move as he went, Bruce helped me stand (fatigue had rendered my legs temporarily uncooperative). He fitted a safety harness around my waist and under my crotch and turned me around to face the cliff.

"Have you ever rappelled before, Gordon?"

"No."

"Well, I'm going to give you a quick course in rappelling."

This was not exactly true. Bless his heart, with his little lie, Bruce was trying to help me save face. This was not rappelling. The truth was I was about to be lowered on a safety line. Anyhow, Bruce told me what I needed to do during our descent to safety. Then, after a short radio conference with the support team above, we started to move over the edge I had earlier considered sliding over. Good thing I didn't. It was 40 feet to the next landing; I'd have broken something for sure.

As Bruce shepherded me down the face of the cliff, he began to praise my progress:

"You're doin' great. You're keeping your legs straight, your feet well apart and your body out, well away from the cliff. You're doing everything exactly as I told you."

What a surprise! Suddenly this lifeguard, 30 years my junior, felt like a nurturing older brother. My spirits began to lift. I was moving

78.

-☼-

from humiliation back to the joy of adventure. I began to fantasize that I was a veteran mountain climber returning, victorious, from some awe-inspiring ascent. Bruce must have sensed my overreaction to his positive reinforcement, because he quickly added:

"You're doing much better than most of the people I rescue off of this cliff."

My fantasy vanished.

Reaching the horizontal surface of the beach was sublime deliverance. Three waiting lifeguards helped me off with the rescue gear. I began to thank them and to apologize for all the trouble I'd caused them.

"Tell him," Bruce said, pointing to a uniformed man sitting behind the wheel of the pickup. I walked over to the truck and met with the lieutenant of the San Diego Lifeguards, at that moment not a happy man. As he took down my name and address, I repeated my apologies and, hoping to avoid a citation, began praising the skills of his rescue team.

"Forget that," he said. *"The important thing is we got you down without injury. And, hopefully, next time you'll know to come down the safe way, which, by the way, is right over there."*

He pointed off to his right. I thanked him one more time, started off toward the surf, then changed my mind. The afternoon's episode had blunted my desire to swim. I was exhausted, both physically and mentally. All I wanted to do was go back to my room and hide. I turned back toward the cliffs. There, off to the right of the lifeguards' truck, not 100 yards south of where I had marooned myself, a trail of rough stairs zigzagged up the cliff's face.

As I lay soaking in a hot bath back in my hotel room, I shook my head at the folly of even having considered sliding over that trough's lower edge into an unknown drop down the cliff's face. I'd come close to risking serious physical injury just to avoid having people I didn't even know learn I'd done something dumb. I was ready to try to cover up one stupid act with an even greater stupidity. That's a ruinous strategy that's brought more than a few people tumbling down to wretched demise. It is so much more sensible to admit having made a mess than to burrow deeper into it.

I thought of how — even though, intellectually, I realize that all of us experience impasse many times in our lives — I had found it so difficult to say that I was stuck. It requires a certain courage to make such an admission.

I mused on how nurturing the experience of my rescue had been for me. Quite a surprise, really. I can only hope that the next time my incorrigible foolishness leads me into an immobilizing dead end, I will find the courage to call out for help.

Ah! Courage, courage, courage. Courage to cross boundaries. Courage to admit idiocy. Courage to acknowledge impasse. Courage to open up to being rescued. We need much courage if we are to respond successfully to the consequences of exploring beyond authorities' sometimes-beneficial, sometimes-detrimental boundaries. And, if we are to grow, explore we must.

Chapter Nine

FIRST THERE'S GROPE, THEN THERE'S ROTE

he was always amazed
and had TIME just
to gaze

Now

...N, t and his

his soul shone like the wind

and he moved like the wind

the top of his head was flung open wide you could see straight inside

his soul shone like gold and could NEVER be sold.

his arms tumbled down

his soul winced and shrunk

even his toes rarely touched down to the ground

In the very beginning, if you think way back

There once was a day.

Then came the day someone casually said...

You should plant both your feet firm on the ground

so he did.

...ned his gaze down ...h of his dar ...nake sure that his ...didnt float off and play.

The door was ajar but not very far

he emptied his thoughts

Sometimes his heart would cry out quite loud

and every so often a tear would go plop

he held his feet in some shoes

2   3   7

0 24100 12843 4

-6-7-   7 6 5 4 3 2 1 +

90°

Someone laughed at him as he sung to the trees...

And so he promised himself never again would he sing to the trees (or the leaves)

but still they laughed

At most everything he did

so he thought to himself it must be more like them

So he watched and he thought what to think what to not

walk like i walk
talk like i TALK
dont fiddle
work hard
dont be late
dont sigh
dont cry
lookem' smack in the eye
stand up straight
dont do this
dont do that

One day, back when I was still at Hallmark, Peg Charpentier called from Personnel:

> *"Hi, Gordon. This is Peg."*

> *"Hi, Peg. How's it goin'?"*

> *"I can't complain, really. You know: The treadmill keeps going faster and faster. But it's okay. I'm surviving. How are things with you?"*

> *"Fine."*

> *"You're not going too hard, are you? I worry about you. You need to slow down."*

> *"I will. What's up?"*

> *"Well, are you familiar with the course we give in Corporate Training: 'Management, Concepts and Practices'?"*

> *"Uh-uh."*

> *"Well, it's a series of five workshops Hallmarkers are automatically signed up to take when they're promoted to the level of supervisor."*

> *"Never heard of it."*

> *"Well, they probably didn't have it back when you first made supervisor. That's probably so long ago."*

> (Defensive guffaw) *"Yeah, you're probably right."*

> *"Anyway, it's a series of workshops about various aspects of management, and I was thinking it would be a good idea to have you give some kind of an innovative session at the end*

85.

of the series. A summary of the content of the course. Something really innovative. Something they'd really remember. We could call it 'The Creative Manager' or something like that."

"You want me to create a workshop that you would add to these others?"

"I think it would be a wonderful addition. Something like the sort of thing you've been doing lately."

"And you'd call it 'The Creative Manager'?"

"Something like that. Yes."

"What are the other workshops about?"

"One of them is on performance reviews and salary administration. One is on conducting effective meetings. Another is on business plans and the corporate vision. Um... One is on..."

"Why don't you just send me whatever material you can on all the workshops and let me play with it."

The next day, a thick envelope came in the interoffice mail. It was from Peg. The workshop outlines — all very condensed, all very rational, all very linear. The sort of stuff I've always tried to keep at arm's length.

I plodded through the material, retaining nothing. Dreary stuff. Necessary, I suppose, but dull, dull, dull — like so many of the workshops I'd attended at Hallmark. (I'm sure they are available in abundance in most corporations.) They invariably offer the same promise:

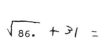

"Follow the steps in this program, and solutions to your workday problems will be within your grasp."

It is a false promise.

If memory served me well, a more common experience, for me anyhow, was to finish a workshop filled with a *step-one-step-two-step-three-voila!-solution!* dogma and return to the world beyond workshops to find a waiting lineup of problems that quickly had me wondering once again:

"<u>Now</u> what the hell is going on?"

This gave me an idea.

I called Peg. Got her voice mail on the first two tries. Got her on the third.

"Peg, I've gone through the material you sent. On the workshops. Dreary stuff."

"Now, Gordon."

"I can't do what you're asking."

"The workshop?"

"Do a workshop that would be a creative recap of all the other workshops in your series. The 'Creative Manager' thing you suggested."

"But..."

"Wait. I'll do the workshop, but I want to call it 'Grope' instead of 'The Creative Manager.' And the object wouldn't be to give ten easy steps to the solution of all management problems. Basically that's what your other workshops claim to do, isn't it?"

"Oh, now, Gordon..."

"Wait, Peg, hear me out. Please. I think a manager's world is not black and white. It's a world filled with uncertainties and dilemmas. The sort of thing that would leave any neophyte moaning, 'What the hell is this?' So I think it would be useful if we could offer your new managers what you might call a 'what-the-hell-is-this' experience in the safety of a workshop environment before they're hurled, unbaptized, into the real thing. If nothing else, it would be a good balance against all those cure-all courses that promise more than they can possibly deliver, create unrealistic expectations and set people up for disillusionment and insipient cynicism.

"So what I'm proposing is a workshop called 'Grope.' The object would be to expose the participants to a three-hour bombardment of nonrational experiences that would leave them wondering, 'What the hell was that all about?'

"After all, groping and wondering what the hell is going on are both important parts of managing, aren't they?"

There was a long silence on the phone. Then, finally:

"Once."

"What?"

"You can do your workshop once."

So we had our workshop: "Grope". The theme of groping precluded a structured agenda. And feeling responsible for the success of an agenda that was intentionally without structure generated considerable

confusion within the group. But, as it became apparent that valuable experiences were emerging from our intentional chaos, the anxiety was displaced by exhilaration. For three hours, the workshop participants lost their balance, recovered it, lost it again, found it again, rolling with the vagaries of transrationality, tasting the heady intoxication of groping with abandon. Time flew by. The session came to its end. People were leaving. And sure enough, many of them were mumbling to themselves some equivalent of: *"What the hell was that all about?"*

What it was all about was nonlinearity.

In their book, *The Matter Myth*, Paul Davies and John Gribbin write:

"In physics, a linear system is, simply speaking, one in which the whole is equal to the sum of its parts (no more, no less), and in which the sum of a collection of causes produces a corresponding sum of effects. ...The very concept of scientific "analysis" depends on this property of linearity — that understanding the parts of a complex system implies understanding the whole. ...The success of linear methods over the past three centuries has, however, tended to obscure the fact that real systems almost always turn out to be nonlinear at some level. When nonlinearity becomes important, it is no longer possible to proceed by analysis, because the whole is now greater than the sum of its parts. Nonlinear systems can display a rich and complex repertoire of behavior, and do unexpected things — they can, for example, go chaotic. Without nonlinearity, there would be no chaos, because there would be no diversity of possible patterns of behavior on which the intrinsic uncertainty of nature could act."

In our Grope workshop we had left our habitual corporate culture's analytical, explicit, rational, concrete, goal-oriented, linear reality where *"the whole is equal to the sum of its parts (no more, no less)"* and had experienced a brief expedition into an alternate reality — diffuse, spontaneous, playful, holistic, non-linear — where *"the whole is now greater than the sum of its parts."* That surplus over and above *"the sum of its parts"* was creative energy. And it left the workshop participants — denizens of corporate linearity — wondering:

"What the hell was that all about?"

Ah! Success!

Peg called a couple of days later.

> *"Gordon, your Grope workshop got really good evaluations. Would you like to give it again?"*

> *"Sure."*

I felt disappointed at my sense of relief over receiving good evaluations. (I have always wanted my acts of rebellion — and the Grope workshop had been such an act — to be met with approval and, at the same time, I have always been disappointed when such approval is bestowed.)

We scheduled a time and date for the next Grope. I marked it on my calendar and promptly forgot about it until the day before. At the end of that day, I pulled out the file of written material I had gathered from the first Grope session and prepared for the next morning's workshop.

The second Grope wasn't exactly a dud, but it sure lacked the energy of the first session. That didn't really catch my attention, though, because there was plenty else on my plate at the time.

A month or two later, Peg called me again. Time to do another Grope workshop. Okay. I marked it on my calendar. Again, late in the afternoon before the scheduled day, I went to my file cabinet and pulled out my Grope material. And, finally, it occurred to me:

"Wait a minute! This isn't groping. This is... formula."

In our first Grope session, because we had been willing to flow without structure, to remain unattached to outcome, we opened ourselves to the creative energy that is extruded from chaos and found a *"diversity of possible patterns of behavior."* Then, because I was so enamored by the exhilaration of that creative energy, I seized upon the elements of our experience and made a formula out of them. I took that formula (my Grope material) to the second workshop where, consequently, the experience became structured rather than fluid, linear rather than non-linear, formulary rather than seminal. I was no longer facilitating a Grope session; I was conducting a *rote* session.

Rote has nothing to do with creativity.

The next morning, I told the new group of workshop participants what I had discovered. And, with their enthusiastic support, I threw my notes into the wastebasket. Rote vanished, Grope returned, along with the original scariness and energy. By letting go, we regained what had been lost. At the second session, when I unwittingly shifted the workshop from Grope to Rote, I had opened a door that allowed the re-entry of what might be thought of as organizational entropy. I looked up the definition of entropy in the dictionary. It read:

> **en′trô·py,** *n.* **[Gr.** *entropia, entrope,*
> **a turning toward] the degradation of**
> **matter and energy to an ultimate state**
> **of inert uniformity.**

Wow! That could be a definition for bureaucracy!

It is a common history of enterprises to begin in a state of naive groping, stumble onto success, milk the success with a vengeance and, in the process, generate systems that arrogantly turn away from the source of their original success: groping.

If an organization is to choose vigor over "*an ultimate state of inert uniformity*," it must honor and support both the rational exploitation of success and the nonrational art of groping.

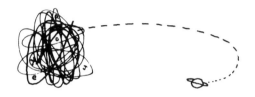

Rote is Hairball.   Grope is Orbiting.

Chapter Ten

CONTAINERS CONTAIN

A jug, a box, a bucket, a bottle. They have in common that they are all containers.

For a moment, take your mind back to a time when there were no human-made containers. There was such a time:

Picture a prehistoric family whose home is a cave. Just outside the mouth of the cave is a spring-fed stream. Any time members of the cave clan are thirsty, all they have to do is take the few short steps from the cave to the stream, drop down on their hands and knees, lower their faces to the water and drink. Convenient. But dangerous. Watering places have always been dangerous places when there are marauding carnivores searching for a meal. A human being, head down, drinking water makes vulnerable prey.

One morning, as the sun rises, the matriarch of this long-ago family awakens from a deep sleep. She is thirsty. Slowly she stands, stretches, moans not unpleasurably and turns toward the stream to drink. Just as she emerges from the mouth of the cave, the morning silence is broken by a throaty growl. Fear pulls her back into the safety of the cave, its entrance guarded by a small fire. She waits. And waits.

Eventually, her growing thirst overcomes her fear. Once more she emerges from the cave, carefully scanning the tangled beauty of the danger-filled terrain. Moving silently to the stream, she crouches at its edge. Bending to drink, she sees her wavering reflection watching her and remembers her younger sister, lost to a meat-eater as she bent similarly to drink not long ago. The matriarch straightens and, obeying some quiet impulse, slides her hands into the gentle current of the stream. Palms up, fingers slightly curved, each pressed firmly against the next, she brings her hands together and lo! lifts water to her mouth. All the while watching for danger.

Her thirst quenched, she returns to the haven of the cave to sit and wonder at what it is she has just done. She studies her hands, cups them, uncups them. Again and again. Then:

"What a breakthrough! I have just invented the container!"

Gazing at her cupped hands, she makes plans:

"I will take clay and fashion hands like these, bake them hard in the fire, then fill my clay-cupped-hands with water and keep it in the cave. Then none of us will need to risk death every time we feel thirst."

Her mind takes another leap:

"Then I will make another clay-cupped-hands and keep bobby pins in it and stuff like that."

So it was that the human-made container was first created. And the inventor was right when she said it was a breakthrough. The ubiquitous container has proved to be one of our most enduring and widely-used inventions. Too widely used, in fact. Today we put everything in containers. Even people. Even ourselves.

Imagine: You've just been hired by the corporation of your dreams. It's your first day on the job. You come bounding in, all excited about making a unique and valuable contribution. You are ready to fly when...

BAM!...   You run into an invisible wall.

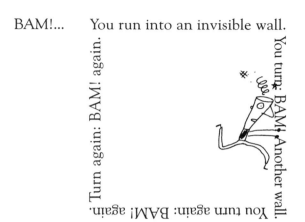

You are confined. Contained in a box called job description. Intended to make you accountable and containable, more often than not its net effect is to restrict you.

Some may protest:

"Wait a minute! We need job descriptions. Without them everyone would be tripping over everyone else."

Not so if we learn to *dance* together. On a dance floor, people are not boxed in, and they manage very nicely to avoid tripping over one another. If we are to achieve the quantum leaps the future seems to be demanding of us, we must risk to leave our containers-turned-cages and find the grace to dance without stepping on toes.

Others' or our own.

Chapter Eleven

CAGE DWELLERS

DATE: September 8, 1990

PLACE: The Sunday Comics

Garfield, leaping, Rambo-like, through the open door of a pet shop, announces himself: **FREEDOM FIGHTER!**

He charges through the shop, flinging open the cages of the confined pets, proclaiming: **YOU'RE FREE! YOU'RE FREE!**

But, instead of rejoicing in this sudden gift of liberation, the cats and dogs and birds all remain in their open cages, intimidated by the unknown possibilities that come with freedom.

Seeing this, Garfield surmises: **HMMM, FOLKS MUST NOT BE HEAVILY INTO FREEDOM THESE DAYS**

Ever flexible, he whirls back through the pet shop, slamming cage doors and cheering: **YOU'RE SECURE! YOU'RE SECURE!**

The pets, reconfined, look relieved.

Same thing happens in the world of people. Many of us choose security over freedom to such an extreme that we confine ourselves and profoundly limit our experience of life. I might surrender to a craving to be secure by electing to live out my life in a closet. Maximum safety, minimum existence.

On the other hand, what if I had a passion for unbridled freedom and the high excitement of living fully? My rambling reverie might run like this:

"Oh, freedom! Elusive freedom! Where might I find your thrill? To soar like a bird unfettered by the brutal bonds of earth. Like a bird... like a bird... That's it!... I'll take up skydiving!"

I check the Yellow Pages. Make the call. Sign up for the training required to jump out of an airplane.

It is a beautiful Sunday afternoon. My ground training is behind me, and I'm on my way in a Cessna 182 up to 3,500 feet to make my first jump. With me are two other students, the jump master and the pilot.

All too soon we are on jump run.

"Door!"

... the jump master yells above the roar of the engine, just before he opens the door. The jump begins. I am amazed at the ease with which the others tumble out into the cloudless sky. Now it is my turn. Hands and feet braced against the doorway, the wind sucking the air out of my lungs, I look down at the neat patterns of tiny farms far below. I begin to have second thoughts. Do I really want *this* much excitement in my life? My reevaluation is interrupted by the jump master, who, behind me, encourages me out the door — out into floorless terror.

My mind screams at me:

"You wanted more freedom, more excitement in your life.
Well, you've sure got it! Big time!"

The rush is incredible. I have a breathtaking sense of being alive... not sure for how long, but a tremendous sense of being alive.

Miraculously, my parachute opens and I drift gracefully down to a safe landing. What a buzz! That part of me that is always on the lookout for something new to become addicted to is immediately hooked. Every Sunday for the next six months, I'm back for another excitement hit.

It is now the first weekend of the seventh month. And here I am, making my third jump of the day, plummeting freestyle in an 1800-foot, 120-mile-an-hour freefall towards earth. The wind rages at my jump suit. As the Kansas landscape zooms up towards me, I find myself thinking:

"I wonder what's for dinner."

Wait a minute! What happened to the excitement? Where did the life-expanding thrill of my first jump go?

Nothing lasts.

Nothing.

I refuse to accept the loss. I've got to recreate the mind-blowing intoxication of my earlier jumps. But how?

A little voice inside me whispers:

"Unbuckle your parachute."

I'm so impatient to get the old excitement back that I seize upon this idea without really thinking it through. Fighting the wind, I reach down with both hands, unbuckle the straps across my chest, worm my way out of the harness, and hurl the parachute away from me.

It works! The excitement quotient skyrockets! Every molecule in my body is screaming:

"Freeeeeeeeeeee e ! "

And then...

SPLAT!

I don't live to share the experience with anyone.

So: Sky diving without a parachute is suicide.
      Total freedom is suicide.

And: Holing up in a closet is vegetating.
      Total security is vegetating.

Somewhere between the ridiculous extremes of vegetating and suicide is the right place for each of us. I've got a feeling that right place is different for you and for me. A different place for different times of our lives and different parts of our lives. Generally, though, my suggestion is, if you want to live more fully, start somewhere toward the safe end of the security/freedom continuum and move mindfully, ever so mindfully, toward the free end.

CHECK
This
OUT

Personals 502

RARE FLIGHT

DEPART FROM: Devious Dependency

DESTINATION: High Triumph

Not the plundering triumph of machismo where the game is to crush a brother or a sister to become the victor of the day — tomorrow's distinguished prey. Not *that* triumph. There is no deliverance there. Not that triumph, but the triumph of finding your divine humanity. To be divinely human — profoundly, passionately human — you must dare to forsake the fearfed grappling for security that enslaves your spirit. Say, "Goodbye, dependency!" Unfold your wings. Brave skyward to the sanctity of grace, whole in the knowledge that — though the mud of your beginnings will soon reclaim you — you are living your moment, heart and soul.

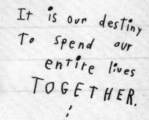

Dwelling in the little bone house on top of your body

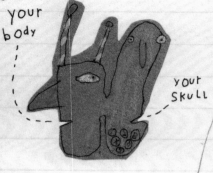

your Skull

NOTICE MY BROTHER'S MULTIPLE NAVELS. THAT'S where There once were multiple umbilical cords, through which came nurturing of the BLACK— and—WHITE sort: Deductive Reasoning, concrete Thinking, Rational Analysis— ALL of it MOTHER's Milk TO MY Brother.

→

↓

BROTHER spends all his Waking hours Punching his BUTTons.

According To The ORder in WHich I PUSH MY BUTTons, I COME UP WiTH ANswers of which I am very certain.

WELL, YOU KNOW WHAT
IT'S LIKE WHEN YOU'RE
CERTAIN OF SOMETHING.
YOU'RE MORE inclined TO
WANT TO SHARE it.
MY BROTHER LOVES to share.
     JUST LISTEN TO him: ------

(punch! punch! punch!)
NO, we can't do That. It's not
        COST - EffecTive.
(PUNCH! punch! Punch!)
Yes, That would be an acceptable
course of action. we've done That
BEFORE and it's worked satisfactori
    (Punch! punch! punch!)
well, Now, we've never Tried That
BEFORE. we'd better TAKE That
      idea under advisement.

Judgement after
   Judgement
after Judgement
after Judgement,
all based on
   past history. - - - - - -

MY SISTER has
No navels.
No BUTTONS.
NONE at all.
NEVER has.

But i do have ANTENNa,
Through which I
Receive The Intelligence
Of The
UNIVERSe.

don't
Start.

THERE ARE UNLIMITED
TRUTHS outside of our
CONSENSUS Reality,
just waiting
to come in.

SNOrt!

Most, if not all,
of Our shared
Knowledge Was
once outside The Ring
of Our Awareness.

- sheesh!

And A Primary Path
for New Information
into OUR consciousness
IS THROUGH MY Antenna.

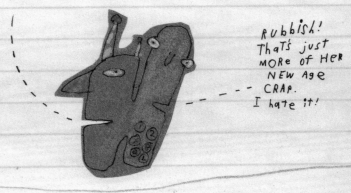

Rubbish!
That's just
MORE of HER
NEW Age
CRAP.
I hate it!

THE FACT IS, MY BROTHER Lives iN conTinuing
ANXieTY That I'll Recieve SOME PROFOUND
NEW INFORMATION through my antenna,
SAY iT OUT LOUD and EmbaRRass him.
You see, he cannoT deal with any
information THAT
HAS NoT BeeN
VERified,
CoNFiRmed and
Accepted by the
ESTABLISHMEnT.

QUITE LOGICALLY, what ~~I~~ I DO TO PROTECT **YOU** FROM THE DANGER of being discredited by my SPACEY SISTER is to REACH my hand across and Cover up HER MOUTH.

mmph! mmph!

So! Even inside our heads there is a guardian of the Hairball. Oh well, it's a necessary function, I suppose. But what a pity the left twin has been taught to carry it out so tyrannically, muffling his sister's originality in order to feel secure in the established order of things.

If we are to make ourselves more fully available to the unfathomable potential of our **whole** mind, we must unmuzzle the genius of the right twin.

How might we do that?

So many books and workshops that promise to increase our capacity for creativity fail to deliver because they prescribe removing the left twin's censoring hand through rational means. That won't work. To take a rational approach to halting the left twin's silencing of the right twin is to play directly into his strength, which is rational thinking. And you cannot beat him at his own game. Ultimately, the only effective way to remove his inhibiting hand is through *trans*rational thinking.

On-the-other-side-of-rational/above-and-beyond-rational thinking.

So how do we ungag Original Thought transrationally? By soaring above the rational on the wings of spiritual intuition. Poetry.

Art.

Myth.

Magic.

Play.

Imagination.

Chapter Thirteen

ABOUT TEASING

A manager in Management Information Systems at Hallmark had invited me to conduct a workshop on creativity for the people in his section. He had reserved a meeting room in the Hyatt Hotel next door to Hallmark's headquarters in midtown Kansas City.

On the appointed morning, I arrived at 8:30, half an hour before we were scheduled to begin, so that I might have time to arrange my materials and otherwise prepare for the group's arrival. Precisely at 9:00, about 25 people entered the room. Although I'm sure they had walked over from Hallmark's main building, which was just across the square, they looked as if they had arrived by tour bus. In single file, three feet apart, they shuffled obediently to their seats.

All the men had on dark blue or grey pin-striped suits, white shirts and conservative ties. About a third of the women were wearing solid, navy blue suits, white blouses and one variation or another of those product-management bow ties. The rest had on tastefully tailored business dresses.

They'd have fit in beautifully at IBM or some like corporation... except for one thing: They were all wearing goofy hats — each of them different. I remember, in particular, one woman wearing a fire fighter's hat with all sorts of plastic fruits and vegetables stuck on it. She looked like the spirit of Carmen Miranda reincarnated — but without the energy.

None of the group displayed any real energy. The incongruity of the suits and the crazy hats was not generating the good humor one might expect. Instead, wooden smiles and just-as-wooden postures suggested the synthetic aliveness of corporate marionettes. I thought:

"Ahhh... we're having mandatory fun."

Mandatory fun is the force-feeding of some cockeyed activity to a captive audience with intent to generate joviality. Almost without exception, these ill-advised intrusions fail to create the mirth they are intended to. The result is a discomfort that everyone feels, but no one acknowledges.

I felt a certain sympathy for these victims of obligatory happiness and invited them to take their hats off if they wished. They did so instantly, which tended to confirm my suspicions that they had been intruded upon emotionally. Suddenly it became very important to me not to infringe further. That resolve was to serve me well during our very first exercise.

Because Hallmark owns Binney & Smith, which makes Crayola Crayons, one of the perks I enjoyed at Hallmark was full access to all the wax crayons I wanted. That morning I had brought along with me a cardboard carton filled with 300 or 400 loose crayons, which I dumped on the floor, saying:

> *"Help yourself to whatever colors you want. Pick up a sheet of paper from this pile. Make yourself comfortable anywhere in the room. And make marks on paper that have something to do with who-you-are and Management Information Systems and Hallmark."*

(I used the phrase *marks on paper* advisedly. The word *drawing* has inhibiting performance expectations attached to it. An invitation to make marks on paper is less likely to be intimidating.)

The general commotion of the group busying itself with selecting crayons gave way to a meditative silence as people settled in around the room and focused on their task. Sitting in the quiet, I wondered what was going on in these individuals' minds. Some seemed rapt;

others, lost. I hoped that none would see this exercise as simply one more foolish intrusion to be suffered silently.

After a while, when people were finishing, sitting back, gazing at their work or around the room, and starting quiet conversations, I asked if anyone in the group would be willing to risk sharing with the rest of us what he or she had put on paper.

Everyone went into invisible mode.

All eye contact ceased. Suddenly every person in the group was checking his or her fingernails for crayon wax. The message was clear:

"No. We don't want to share."

Had I not been so touched by the spiritually dampening effect of the silly-hat fiasco, I think I might have been tempted to coax someone to show the rest of us what he or she had done. After all, how could we explore creativity without risking and sharing?

But, when it's coming from a workshop leader, coaxing is a hair's breadth from coercion. And coercion is a deterrent to creative participation.

And a workshop without creative participation is not a creative workshop at all, but rather an exercise in cultural indoctrination.

There must be no coaxing from me in *this* workshop.

I let it go:

"Nobody want to share? Okay, let's move on."

But as I began describing the next activity, I happened to notice a woman toward the back of the room who was making what I would describe as intentional eye contact with me. It was an inviting stare that seemed to say:

"If you will give me personal encouragement, I will share my drawing with the group."

I responded to her cue:

"You wouldn't by any chance be willing to show us what you did in that last exercise?"

Without a word, the woman popped out of her chair and, with a bashful eagerness, walked directly to the flip chart at the front of the room. There, on the large newsprint pad, she began cheerfully tracing out what I presumed to be an enlargement of her original drawing. She had not drawn more than three or four lines before one of her co-workers began to tease her about the level of her drawing skill. Others quickly added to the barbs. A rowdy taunting ensued. There was a stunning shift in the woman's energy from one of delighted sharing to a shame-faced defensiveness. After an apologetic explanation of her drawing, she scurried, eyes down, back to her seat.

Back to the safety of the anonymity of the group.

I felt heartsick:

"Wait a minute! What just happened here? I want to talk about this.

"But first I have to give you some of my personal background. I was once an alcoholic. My rehabilitation process included attending various support groups where, over time, I began to find out about some of the many lurking intricacies of addictive behavior. One especially valuable revelation for me was to learn about the powerful role shaming plays in the dynamic of any family cursed by an addiction-poisoned environment.

"Addictive behavior does not damage just the addict, but the

addict's family as well. In an effort to survive the insane behavior of the addicted one, other family members develop reciprocating insanities. And pretty soon, the whole tribe is participating in a jumbled web of addiction-induced craziness. The craziness seduces every family member into compulsively controlling every other family member so that nobody gets any big ideas about breaking the web of madness in some rebellious effort to move toward healthier behavior.

"This compulsion to control, engendered by the addiction, becomes a protector of the addiction. The controlling takes many forms, one of which is shaming.

"We were discussing all this at group one evening when the guy sitting next to me observed, 'Teasing is a disguised form of shaming.'

"Bull's eye! One of the long-locked doors in my mind burst open.

"For as far back as I could remember, I had always been a frenzied teaser but had never looked at why. Now I knew. I teased to control. Why would I want to control? Because I am afraid. For whatever reason, I have had a long-standing fear of others. One way of dealing with this fear was to learn the skill of teasing. I learned it well, eventually walling myself off with a bristling armor of barbed banter designed to blunt the power of those countless people I felt threatened by. My teasing became a weapon intended to push others off balance and thus reduce the sense of menace in my life.

"I have a sinking feeling that the teasing you bombarded your colleague with just now reflects a similar strategy. I suspect that, when you teased this woman, it was an unconscious

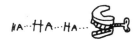

HA···HA···HA···

effort to control her by throwing her off balance — to stop her
from risking, which she was most clearly beginning to do. Why
would you want to do that? Well, when one of us finds the
courage to risk to grow — to leave the status quo of the
Hairball — that can be pretty threatening for the rest of us to
witness. The threat is that we, too, might be expected to grow.
And sometimes growing can be a frightening and painful
experience. If we feel we have already suffered too much pain
or are already frozen by a sense of menace, we are liable to do
anything we can to avoid the pain or threat that often comes
with the experience of growth. So we contrive to stop others in
our loop who display a desire and willingness to grow. One
way to stop them is to shame them. But because we don't
want to admit to others or ourselves that we are trying to stop
growth, we disguise our shaming as teasing — 'all in a spirit of
good fun.' ('Whatsa matter, can'tcha take a little joke?'
— more shaming.)

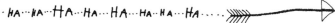

"If I am wrong about this, forgive me. But I think that when
you teased your co-worker about the level of her drawing
ability, you were holding up a stop sign that said:

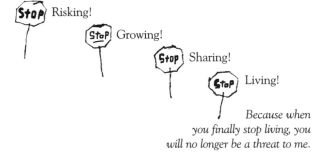

Stop Risking!

Stop Growing!

Stop Sharing!

Stop Living!

*Because when
you finally stop living, you
will no longer be a threat to me.*

"None of us deserves stop signs like that. So I would ask you — those of you who are inclined to tease others — the next time you are about to tease someone, pause for just a moment. Look deep inside yourself. See if you can get in touch with your motivation. And, perhaps, reconsider."

A few days after the workshop, I received an anonymous note thanking me for being aware of what was going on that morning.

The whole experience was so meaningful to me that I recounted the story in the presentations that I was then beginning to give around the country. A man came up to me after one such presentation and thanked me for the "teasing story," as he called it. He said it meant a lot to him because he and his wife and his son used to tease his daughter relentlessly until one day she had tried to commit suicide. Fortunately, she did not succeed at killing herself, but she did succeed in getting her family's attention. They all went packing to a therapist, with the daughter as the designated patient. Before long, the family learned that every time they had teased the daughter, they had been cutting a little more at her self-regard until eventually the accumulation of all the little cuts added up to a wound so painful that she simply wanted to die. To escape through death.

Death of a Thousand Cuts. That is what teasing can be.

The man's lesson was so moving that I added it to my stable of stories. Some time later, when I was telling his tale to another group, someone in the audience protested:

"Wait a minute. Teasing is how I show affection."

My response was:

"You must find a better way."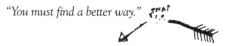

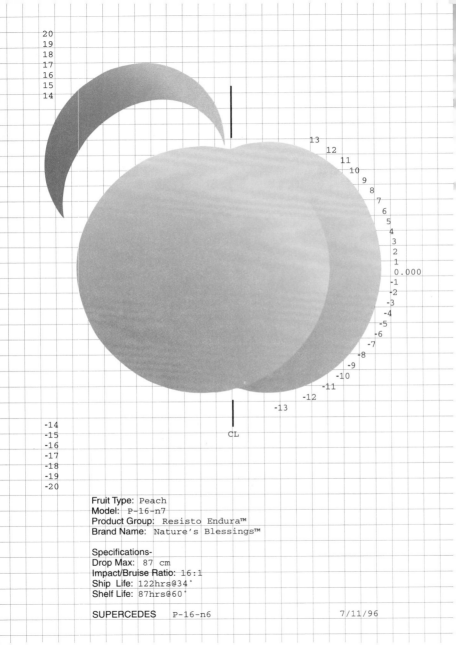

Fruit Type: Peach
Model: P-16-n7
Product Group: Resisto Endura™
Brand Name: Nature's Blessings™

Specifications-
Drop Max: 87 cm
Impact/Bruise Ratio: 16:1
Ship Life: 122hrs@34°
Shelf Life: 87hrs@60°

SUPERCEDES   P-16-n6   7/11/96

Chapter Fourteen

HIGH-TECH PEACHES

What ever happened to *really* juicy peaches? They seem all but gone from the scene. Mostly all you can buy are the high-tech peaches painstakingly developed through the wonders of modern horticultural manipulation. A hardy durability and uniformity of size and shape have been bred into this contemporary generation of peaches to render them better able to survive the rigors of mass marketing.

The juicy peaches of yesterday had a delicacy about them and needed to be handled with care. There is no room for such pampering in today's bruising race from orchard to supermarket. So today's peaches must be tough. And tough they are. But — surprise! — when the toughness was bred into them, the tenderness was bred out, along with the juice and flavor. Such are the priorities of today's competitive world.

What a loss!

I remember, as a kid, coming into possession of a large, ripe peach. While today's peaches seem devoid of fuzz, this one wore a lip-tickling, diaphanous velvet coating that was — even taking into account the tendency of the memories of childhood to magnify the size of everything — easily an eighth-of-an-inch thick. There was juice to spare in that peach — plenty extra to go squirting down my chin as my teeth sliced easily through the delicate skin and into the luscious flesh. A flavor nothing short of erotic exploded in my mouth.

What innocent ecstasy. It's an ecstasy not readily available today. The durability of high-tech has brought to peaches the flavor of pasteboard. You bite into one and think:

> *"This is not a peach! This is some sort of ingenious synthetic substance cleverly pressed into the shape of a peach."*

What a loss, indeed.

This sad state of lost juiciness is echoed in the world of business. There, a monomania for tough-minded, cold-blooded *competitive correctness* has bred the spiritual sensuousness out of most of our human enterprises. That leaves us with a reality of synthetic personas and pasteboard passions, an epidemic of barren careers and a wasteland of workplaces devoid of flavor.

♌

A friend and colleague, David Albright, and I were once asked to create a video dramatizing the ongoing evolution of Crown Center, an office, retail, entertainment, and residential complex in midtown Kansas City. The content of the script presented to us was interesting, but we wanted the final video to be more than that. We were aiming to create something captivating, flavorful — even, you might say, juicy. So we went to considerable lengths to invest the video with appealing camera angles, on-camera activity, dynamic editing and an inviting sound track. There were to be no "talking heads" here. Our efforts to produce a zestful presentation were met with easy success until it came time to add the voice-overs. We wanted a woman's voice for the general narration. And we would need a man's voice giving directions to Crown Center by automobile while, on-camera, the grime-encrusted hand of a supposed service station mechanic pointed to alternate routes on a city map.

David, being the audio/visual specialist, lined up the talent for this part of the production. We all met at a local sound studio, went over the script and chatted about the tone we were looking for. It was important to me that the quality of the voices be conversational to keep the overall mood of the video casual and real. This was not an audition. Ours was not a big enough job to merit auditions. We were just going to go with the woman and man David had brought in.

The woman went first. Although I have seen sound studios depicted in movies, the actual, in-the-flesh experience was new for me. I felt the joy of a kid being allowed to sit in on some cool operation not usually available to the general public. The woman, script in hand, stood at a microphone in a soundproof room of her own. On the other side of a giant picture window in a dimly lit control room, David and I were seated in pamperingly comfortable real-leather swivel chairs.

To the right of David sat a sound expert. I know he was an expert. He would have to be to understand the galaxy of dials, knobs, gauges and switches that was spread out in front of us like some extravagant electronic buffet. I expected Captain Kirk to walk in at any moment.

We all wore earphones — not the little twirpy sponge rubber things that come with a lot of walking audio-cassette players, but real earphones. These were earphones that *enveloped* the ears. I think they were upholstered in leather, too. Soft, pliable leather. The folks at this sound studio believed in indulging their clients. Perhaps all sound studios are like that. I don't know.

Taking her cues from our video, playing on a TV monitor, the woman began to read her narration. It was awful. Well, actually, it was perfect. That's why it was awful. We didn't want perfect. I had tried to tell her that. Perfect is not real. Perfect is not interesting. We wanted real. Conversational. Imperfect. Authentic. It was very hard to get this across to what turned out to be our professional announcers.

No, that's not right. They understood right away. What was hard for them was to let go of their announcer training and be *real.* They both eventually rediscovered their authentic voices, but not before we heard take after take of flawless readings that were all, alas, devoid of the taste of humanness.

How do we become so bogus? Well, our artificiality is caused, in part, by the many teachers and trainers who work so hard to instill a professionalism that prizes correctness over authenticity and originality. Flesh-and-blood students persevere the rigors of broadcast school only to emerge with voices as unreal as their pancake make-up. Budding designers, capable of passion, sweat the grind in schools of architecture and graduate to create environments unconnected to the lusciousness of life. Diamonds-in-the-rough enter business schools and come out the other end as so many polished clones addicted to the dehumanizing power of classification and systematization.

Good news on the peaches, though! It has been reported that at least some horticulturists have come to their senses and are now working to breed the juiciness and flavor back into the bounty of our gardens. In doing so, they will help renew human sensuousness.

Sensuousness has to do with the senses. And it is through our senses that we are able to experience the world around us. So, to the degree that horticulturists succeed in bringing natural flavor back into fruits and vegetables, they will be helping us get back in touch with the natural juiciness of our primal genius.

Perhaps some fine morning, the designers of our work spaces and the setters of our corporate priorities will find the wisdom to follow the lead of those newly enlightened horticulturists, take up the banner of professional sensuousness and begin in earnest the quest for the flavor so long gone from our bread and butter.

Chapter Fifteen

MILK CANS ARE NOT ALLOWED

Somewhere in mid-career at Hallmark, I was bitten by the Corporate Ambition bug. It was my first time, so it hit me pretty hard. I even went out and bought a suit. Here's the story: I had been having a rollicking, productive time in the Contemporary Design department, working with a bunch of eccentric artists and writers to create all sorts of humor products, when I was asked by my long-time boss, mentor, and protector, Bob McCloskey, if I would be willing to head up a tiny, voice-in-the-wilderness department called Creative Licensing. I agreed, on the condition that I be allowed also to continue with my absorbing projects in Contemporary. No problem. The deal was struck.

Very shortly after that, Hallmark's perennial competitor, American Greetings, came out with a cutsie character named Strawberry Shortcake,® which quickly became a red-hot property in the world of character licensing. The sweet little thing began appearing on every legitimate children's product you could imagine, with American Greetings getting its cut on every sale.

Big bucks.

SNIP

All of a sudden, Hallmark's movers and shakers became very interested in licensing. The fledgling Creative Licensing Department staff mushroomed from three to 33. I was sucked right out of my comfy old home in Contemporary Design into the hastily created Hallmark Properties division and put under another, much more intense boss. Broad hints were made that if I could cut it, I'd be promoted to design director — as high as you could go on the Creative side at Hallmark without becoming a vice president. (That's when I went out and bought the suit.)

All sorts of grandiose business plans and money started flying around and the pressure to generate lots of income — *lots* of income — from licensable characters skyrocketed. In the meantime, I had

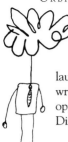

launched into a la-la grandiosity of my own, cornering any artist or writer who would listen to my rhapsodizing over what I saw as an opportunity to achieve a quality and richness comparable to the Walt Disney Studios of the 1930s. I was terribly naive.

Hallmark Properties had become the hot career fast track. Fierce, self-serving, overnight empire-building was under way. Career-obsessed predators who had moved into this alluring new arena were making some mighty ostentatious fiscal promises to top management. To fulfill those promises, staff had to generate great volumes of business. Accordingly, folks on the business side of the Properties Division were slapping Hallmark characters indiscriminately on any non-Hallmark product they could snag. Volume was the name of the new game. Prior to that time, quality had been the game. I was unable to make the switch. The 17 years I had spent in the protective cocoon of Contemporary Design had left me ill-prepared to cope with the harshness of the corporate turpitude that was churning into my life. I found myself thrashing around in a personal career crisis that had me ranting impotently against our abandonment of quality and good taste. At the same time, enchanted by the idea of becoming a design director, I was scrambling to achieve my immediate management's get-rich-quick goals and, in the process, was seriously abusing the talented artists and writers who reported to me.

The part of me that is *total jerk* came to the fore. In my anxiety to measure up, I lost all sense of reasonable expectations and began to deal with my colleagues as if they were threats or, worse, as means to an end. To their great credit, a few of the people I was abusing challenged my behavior. That they each confronted me in such a loving, caring way made it possible for me to see the validity of their complaints. I was filled with a crushing emotional distress that sent me careening to a psychotherapist for help.

This was my first visit to a psychologist, and I brought to it a history of having long scorned anyone in therapy as being either cowardly or self-indulgent. What a difference need makes; now I couldn't get in to see the therapist fast enough. After a few visits, I achieved a certain limited clarity and resolved to remove myself, one way or another, from the cesspit of my torment — my irreconcilably toxic work environment.

I surveyed Hallmark in search of a department to jump to. But, in my state of mind, I could find little promise in any of our Creative areas. Leaving the company was not an option then. I did not yet have the courage to let go of the remarkable financial security that Hallmark had so long provided for its employees. Desperate, I turned to fantasy and conjured a make-believe department that would be ideal to me: a creative-friendly oasis where it would be possible to thumb one's nose at empire building, ass covering, and all those other deterrents to fashioning vigorous concepts and fresh products. With a cleansing sense of excitement, I translated this fantasy of paradise-within-a-corporation into a one-page, hand-written proposal to establish a Humor Workshop. Making a *verboten* end-run around my boss, I presented my proposal over lunch to the vice president of the Creative division.

By the end of the luncheon he had made his decision:

"We've got to do it."

A budget was approved, space was found, my flabbergasted boss was informed, and I set up exploratory interviews with each of the 12 artists and writers I'd been allowed to select as the charter members of the new department. Meeting with each of them separately (none of them knew yet who else would be in the department), I said:

"Pretend that the 13 of us are all quitting our jobs at Hallmark. Pretend that we are pooling our money and starting a creative studio called the Humor Workshop. Hallmark will no longer be our employer but will, rather, be our client, our sole client. Because we are now on our own, we can design our environment any way we want. Fantasize what our studio would be like. Conjure in your mind a place so wonderful that, even on weekends, it would be the place you would choose to be over any other.

"Now then, tell me. What would this place be like?"

To invite people to fantasize is to offer them a safe-conduct pass to muse beyond habitual fatalism. The interviews yielded a dazzling variety of ideas for the new area. There was one recurring suggestion: antique, rolltop desks. That led me to decide to design a department around rolltops. I enlisted the services of Donna Livingston, an architect in our Facilities Planning department. With Fred Wolfe of our Purchasing department, we raided every antique store in greater Kansas City.

This is the best way to go antiquing — with a corporate checkbook. Donna and I wound our way through shop after shop. Whenever we'd find a desk that was right for us, we'd give Fred a high sign. He would then bargain with the owner and complete the necessary paperwork.

I told Donna I wanted every person in the department to have a space that offered both a clear statement of personal territory and a sense of privacy, without cutting everyone off from everyone else (as do the energy-blocking cubicles that currently blight the offices of the corporate world). She responded with a delightful concept: To tie in with the desks, we bought an array of stained-glass windows and old

doors with beveled-glass panels from a local salvage company. Using hefty hemp rope, we hung the windows and doors from the ceiling in an arrangement that established individual private/open work spaces. For variety, we had additional doors hinged together in pairs or threes to fashion privacy screens. The result was functionally effective and aesthetically invigorating. I was ecstatic. The fantasy was materializing.

Toward the end of one afternoon's antiquing, I spied a couple of old milk cans in the corner of a shop. It struck me that they'd make charming wastebaskets. (Bad idea, I was to learn later: easy to fill, hard to empty.) I asked the woman who was puttering around behind the counter whether she had more milk cans. She showed me a half basementful. I signaled Fred to negotiate for 13, a move that was to jeopardize my dream-coming-true.

The following Monday, Donna called to inform me we had been summoned to a meeting in Purchasing.

"When?"

"Right now."

"What's it about?"

"Don't know."

"I'll be right there."

I met Donna at the entrance to the Purchasing department. We were ushered into a conference room where five solemn-faced bureaucrats awaited us. *Five.* After the ritual exchange of Hallmark pleasantries, we moved directly to the issue at hand.

"We've been watching your recent flurry of purchase requisitions and are puzzled by one of them, the one for 13 milk cans. What exactly do you need with 13 milk cans?"

The cans had pushed Purchasing's alert button. The requisitions for the desks had passed by without question, as had those for the doors and windows. Hallmark needs desks, doors and windows, so nothing suspicious there. But milk cans? That was another matter.

I explained, at considerable length, the concept of the Humor Workshop. When I concluded, a woman across the table from me — one who, since Donna and I had entered the room, had not looked up from a thick, opened Corporate Manual and stack of forms that turned out to be our purchase requisitions — said, still not looking up:

"These items are not on the list of approved furniture."

All eyes turned toward me. In the silence, a low-grade panic announced itself in my stomach. I re-explained the concept at even greater length, this time with all the feeling and seductive power I could muster.

With her eyes still locked on the open manual and the offending requisitions, my challenger repeated:

"These items are not on the list of approved furniture."

I was going to lose my paradise. I had an enthusiastic green light from a corporate vice president *and* an approved budget, and yet this bureaucrat was going to stop my concept dead in its tracks. She had the authority to do so and, I feared, was about to use it. Anger and frustration of half a lifetime welled up in me. Suddenly, I saw the woman across the table emitting the malevolent aura of... *The Eternal Squelch* — a green-eyed distillation of all the withholders and door-slammers who had so often seemed to stand between me and salvation. I plummeted into an irrational, paralyzing hate and tried to kill her with my eyes. It was all I could think to do.

138.

bonk

ouch

Donna, apparently remaining free of the sort of self-destructive mental contortions I was now enmeshed in, stayed in touch with her own creativity and so was able to offer a way around my imminent head-on collision with bureaucracy:

> *"Hey, I know!"* she flirted with my would-be foe. *"Hallmark has a corporate art collection. Why don't we just classify all these things as antiques, buy them for the art collection and then lend them to the Humor Workshop?"*

Closing her corporate manual, the woman I was so eager to paint as my enemy looked up, smiling brightly:

> *"What a great idea."*

Often things are slow to get through to me. It was not until several weeks after our meeting with the people in Purchasing that it began to dawn on me: When I succumbed to my anger-turned-hate reaction to a fellow Hallmarker, who happened to make her living as a bureaucrat, I was choosing victimhood as my *modus operandi*. In doing that, I was setting myself up to become a prisoner of the Hairball that she was charged to maintain. Donna's creative response saved me from that and taught me a new survival strategy:

> *Any time a bureaucrat*
> > *(i.e., a custodian of a system)*
>
> *stands between you*
> *and something you need or want,*
> *your challenge is to help that bureaucrat*
> *discover a means,*
> > *harmonious with the system,*
>
> *to meet your need.*

It is a strategy that has helped me stay out of many a Hairball.

Afternote:

For the first few weeks following its opening, the Humor Workshop seemed more like an in-house tourist attraction than a high-performance artists' and writers' studio. A continuous stream of curious visitors from other departments dropped by unannounced to see whether there was any truth to the rumors of a funky new enclave plunked down in their sea of grey. Although they were nearly unanimous in their delight over our offbeat haven, a few sightseers were scandalized at what they perceived as an irresponsible lavishing of corporate funds.

"You can't justify spending the kind of money it must've taken to build this Taj Mahal!" one perturbed division vice president complained.

Wrong!

The sterile, assembly-line cubicles, standard at Hallmark, cost, at that time, $4,200 per person. We chose instead to assemble a unique collection of furnishings that both fostered the free-spirited individuality of the staff and promoted the mission of the department: *innovative* generation of product. Cost? Just $3,500 a head. That's $700 less per person than the cubicle route. We had created a richer, more supportive environment for less money. More for less.

What the disapproving vice president saw as troubling evidence of irresponsible spending was, in fact, the sweet dividends of prudent ingenuity.

Chapter Sixteen

THE POWER OF PARADOX

屋檐我来君之

After three golden years in the role of what I might self-deceptively describe as "leader" of a dozen independent-minded creative geniuses in the Humor Workshop, I was invited by my boss at the time to take a new job across the street in the main building of the corporate headquarters — the Big Grey Place. I was so enjoying the funky energy of the Humor Workshop and its location outside the corporate beltway that it is perhaps understandable that I was resistant to this new job offer, which would clearly pull me into the mainstream.

I was especially reluctant to leave the Humor Workshop because my boss could not give me a clear picture of just what my new assignment would entail. I remember his saying something about his wanting me to serve as a "burr in his saddle." Considering the man's reputation, this amounted to an invitation to become devil's advocate to Attila the Hun. Not a career I would seek.

Further, I was wary that this whole thing had less to do with moving me into a new position and more to do with moving me *out* of the Humor Workshop, where my loose-leaf management style was considered by many straight arrows in the Big Grey Place suspect at best.

At one point, in hopes of getting a broader sense of what this new job would involve, I asked my boss if he had a position title in mind.

He responded:

"I was thinking of something like 'aide-de-camp.'"

"I hate that! (There was probably a whining in my voice.) *It sounds militaristic and servile."*

Without hesitation, he responded:

"Well then, you come up with something."

My paranoia hissed in my ear:

"He doesn't care what the job title will be because there won't be anything to do, anyhow."

With that, our meeting ended; and I spent the rest of the afternoon paralyzed with anxiety over my future with the company.

That evening, to escape my stress, I went jogging after dinner. In less than a mile, I was at peace, my mind a blank. Shortly thereafter, without invitation, a single word popped into my head:

PARADOX
(it was in caps)

Feeling inexplicably excited, I turned immediately and raced back home to the tattered dictionary in my studio. Dripping with sweat, I raced my fingers through the L-M-N-Os to P: pad... Pandora... parade... paradox!

As I read the four definitions, I felt a grin cross my face.

"This is what I want to be. This is what I am."

I became electrified... euphoric!

"If they will OK this as my new title, I'll take the job. But I won't tell them that."

First thing the next morning, I photocopied the definition, then scribbled over the actual word *paradox*. At our next meeting, I laid the photocopy on my boss's desk:

"These are the definitions of the word I would like as my job title."

> beyond; *doxin*, opinion] **1**: a statement or proposition that seems absurd, intellectually self-opposing, or contrary to common belief, yet may be true. **2**: a statement that is false because it contradicts itself. **3**: an experience or thing that seems self-contradictory. **4**: a person who exhibits contradictory or inconsistent behavior.

Have you ever tried to determine a word from its definition? (Without the word's letter count?) It's not as easy as it might seem. Being a Thirty-Days-To-A-More-Powerful-Vocabulary freak, my boss saw it as a challenge. But he was unable to guess this word.

I told him:

"The word's 'paradox.'"

"Could we put a modifier on it?"

"Like what?"

"Something like 'Office of the Paradox.'"

"Whoah! The suggestion hasn't been on your desk for more than 10 seconds, and you're already moving to institutionalize it!"

He backed off. He could sometimes be a very reasonable man.

"How about 'Creative Paradox'?"

(We were in the Creative Division at the time.)

"That sounds good. Yes, I like that."

He told me he would run it past his management and get back to me. He did. The title was approved, and I took the job.

And so it was that the following Saturday morning, I was going through the melancholy task of packing my personal belongings into cardboard cartons and lugging them from my beloved Humor Workshop to a little windowless room on the ninth floor of the Big Grey. Change can be depressing.

The following Monday, Hallmark's daily newsletter, *The Noon News*, carried in its "New Responsibilities" feature a one-line announcement of my appointment to the position of Creative Paradox.

> *"Creative Paradox?"* — people were coming up to me after lunch, *Noon Newses* in hand — *"What the heck is that?"*

I had nothing to tell them. I didn't know what it meant, either.

At this point, I need to give you some background:

To thrive, even to survive, Hallmark must continually tap into its primary creative resource — the people of Hallmark. No surprise, then, that woven into the company incantation chanted by Corporate Communications is a call to creativity...

BRING US YOUR ideas   SHaRe YouR insights

The people respond. Magnificently. How to put a number on it? At this writing, there are approximately 6,000 people at Hallmark's headquarters. If, at any one time, just 5 percent of them answer the call to creativity, that translates into 300 people offering innovative thinking to the corporation.

Unfortunately, while the heart of Hallmark sings the virtues of creativity, the company's intellect worships the predictability of the status quo and is, thus, adverse to new ideas. This incongruity creates a common corporate personality disorder: The organization officially lauds the generation of new ideas while covertly subverting the implementation of those same ideas. The consequence is that, on any given day, umpteen people at Hallmark, responding to official corporate invitation, come up with concepts for new methodologies or fresh, original products. Then those ideas, by nature of their newness, are deemed fundamentally unseemly by the same authority conglomerate that asked for them in the first place. This makes for a lot of frustrated ideamongers.

One day, one of these thwarted contributors vented her frustration to a friend. The friend said:

> *"Why don't you take your idea to the Creative Paradox.*
> *He has nothing to do, anyway."*

So the woman looked up my number and called me:

> *"Could I come see you about an idea I have?"*

> *"Sure."*

She came and described her idea for a new product. It was a terrific idea, and I told her so:

> *"That's a wonderful idea. I think we should do it."*

She broke into a grin:

> *"Thanks a lot."*

She left and I remember thinking:

> *"Boy! That was easy."*

She went back to her boss:

"The Creative Paradox thinks my idea is terrific and we ought to do it."

Now an unexpected phenomenon began to emerge. Because *Creative Paradox* had no meaning within the context of the corporate culture, nobody knew exactly where I stood in the power hierarchy. But how much power each player has is important information to those who cultivate their careers politically. And many — especially middle managers — will, when in doubt, play it safe and guess on the high side in the power-estimating game. So a number of people assumed I had more power than I actually had. (In fact, I had none at all.) But as soon as they assumed I had a certain amount of power:

I *had* it.

The woman's boss, perhaps speculating that I might be a person of some power, must have thought:

"If the Creative Paradox supports her idea, maybe I'd better support it, too."

So he did. And her idea became a product. And, lucky for me, it sold.

Soon word got around:

"If you have an idea that is stuck in the system, just call the Creative Paradox."

My phone started ringing off the hook.

To enhance the illusion of my emerging, indefinable (nonexistent) power, I set about to transform my little office into a corporate version of Merlin's Den. A friend in Building Services cut me some long, thin panels of pressed board, which we hung under the overhead fluorescents to block their light. I then lit the now-darkened room with candles and a single drawing board lamp. This gave me sufficient local light to work, but left the room still very dark in contrast to the antiseptic brightness of the rest of the corporate complex. To suggest a sense of the inscrutable, I adorned the walls with great enlargements of Chinese calligraphy and cryptic maxims scrawled on large sheets of newsprint.

From Anne Van Rossum Lawrence, a Hallmark artist, I bought a fanciful sculpture she had fashioned from an antique oak dining-room chair. Painted in brightly-colored zigzags, checks, stripes and waves, the sculpture boasted wide-spread angel wings and sprouted a halo, suspended on a stick attached to the chair's back. *Angel Chair* was the sculpture's name, and I hung it from the ceiling, tilted forward at an angle of about 45 degrees directly above my drawing board chair, hoping to give the impression that I'd recently slid out of it and dropped down to earth.

This is where I would meet with Hallmarkers who had hot ideas stuck in corporate limbo.

Tap Tap Tap. A visitor would peer tentatively through the open door into my darkened room.

Sitting in the candlelight under the suspended *Angel Chair,* I would, through my notion of what method acting is, become the High Lama of Shangri-la as I recalled seeing him played in an old black-and-white Ronald Coleman film, *Lost Horizon.* If I remember correctly, the movie Lama was 136 years old. Frail, gentle and profoundly wise.

I would become 136 years old.

"*Come,*" I would beckon frailly to my visitor.

"*Sit,*" I would whisper, gesturing toward the three director's chairs just inside the door.

We would sit in silence a moment, allowing an air of sacredness to emerge. Then, finally:

"*Tell me,*" I would open.

The visitor would describe the idea.

"*Good idea,*" I would pronounce in a voice copied from a Wise-North-American-Indian character I'd once seen in another movie. (I think it was *Cry of the Wolf.*)

"*Thank you,*" the visitor would smile. And leave. Ratified.

I did that for *three* years. The last three years of my 30 at Hallmark I had no job description and a job title that had no meaning. And yet they were the most enriching, fruitful, productive, joy-filled years of my entire career.

Talk about a paradox.

EXPLOit the absurdities & Embrace the enigmas

Revel in the powers of paradox

Afternote 1:

One time after I'd told my Paradox story at a conference, someone in the audience asked:

"Did you always tell people their ideas were good?"

"Yes."

"Were all the ideas good?"

"Almost all."

"What about the ideas that weren't good?"

"They were almost good."

"Wouldn't that destroy your credibility — saying every idea was a good idea?"

"The person I was visiting with wouldn't know I told everyone else the same thing."

"But why tell someone an idea is good even if it isn't?"

"In any large corporation, rank-and-file workers who put forward truly new ideas have the deck stacked against them right from the beginning. Most companies are peppered with people who are very quick to say 'no.' Most newly hatched ideas are shot down before they even have time to grow feathers, let alone wings. In saying 'yes' to all those who brought their ideas to me, I was simply leveling the imbalance a bit. And it worked. People who have a deep passion for their ideas don't need a lot of encouragement. One 'yes' in a sea of 'no's' can make the difference."

Afternote 2:

Someone in another audience offered the observation:

"These stories you've been telling us... I think you got away with all you did because it was Hallmark. No other company would have put up with the things you did."

As best as I can recall, my response was something like:

"You're probably right. But neither you nor I could know what other things I would get away with at another company until I worked at that company.

"If you saw some of my steel sculptures, you might say to me that the reason I was able to make them was because my medium was steel. And you would be correct. Would you then say that marble would not put up with that sort of thing? You'd be right again. But I would not work with marble in the same way I worked with steel.

"So, too, if I had moved from Hallmark to another company, I would have altered my approach and style in keeping with the shift to a different medium. Why not think of any organization you're a part of as a unique medium in which you have the opportunity to create?"

Chapter Seventeen

DEATH MASKS

Staff meetings were not my first love at Hallmark. You might even say I had a real aversion to them. On one occasion, my boss asked each of the six or seven of us who reported to him to come to our next staff meeting prepared to report on something. Each of us was to fill ten minutes.

I felt immediate anxiety. There was part of me that hated to report on anything I was doing. I was afraid I'd be told either:

or:

"What to do? I know! I'll just report on something that has nothing to do with anything I'm doing." (After all, my boss had not been specific.)

When the next staff meeting was held, and it came my turn to report, I held up a drawing:

"I would like to report on masks."

Silence. Every face at the table went blank.

"My sense of these meetings is that we come into this windowless room, which, I am told, is lit with balanced fluorescent lighting (whatever that is) and is decorated in tasteful corporate greys. We all sit around this long, wooden conference table that always reminds me of the lid of a coffin.

"And everyone has a mask on.

"Now, one of the reasons for our coming together like this is to work together to find more creative responses to the challenges that are hurled at us every day.

"And I've been wondering:

'Why do we meet this way? Surely there must be more promising approaches to finding effective solutions to our problems.'

"The more I thought about it, the more intrigued I became — about the masks, especially. So I thought it might be instructive to ask one of these people with a mask on if we might look behind his mask in hopes of learning something."

This said, I held up another drawing:

Addressing the drawing of the masked face as if it were a real person, I asked:

"Would it be all right with you if, just this once, we removed your mask in hopes of learning what lies behind it?"

(I moved the drawing to cover my face, making it a mask, and spoke as if I were the man in the drawing):

"Well... (haltingly)... *OK... but just this once."*

Moving the drawing away from my face, but still holding it up, I spoke once again as myself, this time addressing the people in the meeting:

"Okay, we have his permission, which is important. But before we remove his mask, notice his almost-twinkling eyes. And his bright, jovial smile. Notice, too, the hand held up as if to say:

'Hi! How ya'll doin'?'

"Just another happy Hallmarker.

"Now, let's remove the mask.

"Behind the cheery facade, we find an expression filled with pain and anxiety. Suddenly, the hand that seemed to be saying 'Hi!' now appears to be pleading:

'Stay away! Don't get too close!'

"Maybe the source of this poor man's anguish is the angry blemish at the side of his nose. This is a ZIT.

"Besides a physical zit, there is such a thing as a corporate zit. And, just like the physical zit, the corporate zit always seems to emerge at the worst possible time.

"Have you ever known anyone to get a physical zit two days into a week-long, solo retreat in the desert or mountains? No way! Zits much prefer to make an appearance the afternoon of the night of the big dance or some important banquet.

"So here you are, getting dressed for a big night out. And as you pass the mirror in the hall you happen to catch a glimpse of your reflection and...

ARRRGH!

"You see this unlovely thing that has arisen from within, blighting the soft curve of your nose and beaming angry red out to a watching world. You dash to the bathroom, fling open the medicine chest and frantically ransack its contents, desperately searching for some magical commercial concoction designed to shrink or at least camouflage such untimely eruptions.

"It's the same way with corporate zits. They pop up at the worst possible time — right before monthly report or your performance review, a surprise audit, or perhaps a visit from a major client. Then there's the same mad scramble to cover up the offending imperfection.

"Well, to have a zit is to be human.

"And to be human is to be less than perfect.

"And, if we are less than perfect, we don't get an A-plus.

"I suspect that many of us still operate under the mistaken notion that if eventually we accumulate enough A-pluses, *they will fill the void that was created by the loss of unconditional love somewhere in our infant past. Fool's errand! All the A-pluses in the universe will not fill that void. It is an emptiness that can only be dealt with from within, through a growing acceptance of self, leading to a healthy love of self.*

"There's a practical side, too, though. An A-plus might be required to get a raise, clinch a promotion, or even keep your job. So, when someone asks, 'How's it going?,' the great temptation is to put on a mask with a fabricated smile and answer with a counterfeit confidence:

> *'Fine, just fine. Everything's under control.'*

"While beneath the mask may lie unrelenting hurt and need.

"Don't get me wrong. I support your right to wear a mask. Masks have real social value in that they allow you privacy and space in an often brutal world. But there is a price you pay for wearing a mask. Masks cause little deaths — little soul deaths. When you wear a mask, nobody (not even you) gets to find out who you really are. When you wear a mask, nobody (not even you) gets to find out what you really need. And when you wear a mask, nobody (not even you) gets to find out what you really have to offer.

"That's a ruinous price to pay for an A-plus."

Most likely I will never know whether my report on masks held any value for my colleagues in that meeting; their masks remained in place. There was a wonderful payoff for me, however: From that day on, I was excused from the torment of attending staff meetings. *(Out of the Hairball!)*

Candor pays.

Chapter Eighteen

THE PYRAMID & THE PLUM TREE

> *The poet's eye, in a fine frenzy rolling,*
> *Doth glance from heaven to earth, from earth to heaven;*
> *And, as imagination bodies forth*
> *The forms of things unknown, the poet's pen*
> *Turns them to shapes, and gives to airy nothing*
> *A local habitation and a name.*
>
> — William Shakespeare, *A Midsummer Night's Dream*

For years, I had been rolling my eyes at corporate looniness in general and Hallmark's cultural convolutions in particular. Then — surprise! — my boss asked me to put some thoughts together as to how Hallmark might more effectively organize itself. Fun assignment! I thought of Hallmark's organizational model, the pyramid. Then of models in general. Then wondered:

"Why models?"

Well, in an effort to cope with the incomprehensibility of infinite reality, we ever-curious, ever-pondering, compulsively controlling Homo sapiens create theoretical models. These models are ingenious beams of speculation that we use to penetrate and define the dark mysteries of boundless existence. Sometimes elegantly structured, usually self-confirming, our models are like the headlights of a car, designed to light our way. Whatever is illuminated becomes our truth, and we organize our lives around it. But this light we create can also blind us. Too often we are blinded into believing that our models are the whole reality, forgetting that they are simply useful fact/fantasy coping devices.

The more fully we believe a model is reality, the more rigid the model becomes. And the more rigid it becomes, the more it confines us. There is a sense of security in this, the sense of security that comes from being contained by the "known" and thus shielded from the threat of the unknown. So the mixed blessing of models is that while they can generate a sense of coherence through a groundedness (in "knowledge"), they can also, if used without mindfulness, become addicting anesthetics to the pain of an inscrutable universe and further insulate us from full reality, which is the realm of infinite possibilities.

Like the overwhelming majority of corporations and similar organizations, Hallmark was firmly grounded in — and securely hobbled by — a deeply embedded belief in the exclusive validity of the pyramid hierarchy model.

"Unh! This is heavy stuff," I thought and started sliding into heavy-thinking mode.

Big Mistake.

"Hold it!" I stopped myself. *"If I get heavy about this, I'll be running the same trampled track that so many runners better than I have run before me. And I'll probably end up at the unimaginative dead end of the bottom line. It would be a better use of my time to lighten up and leave the heavy thinking to the heavy thinkers."*

Thus freed, I whipped out a legal pad and started to play.

Try to suspend judgment as you follow along. This is, after all, just exploratory sport with "imagination the rudder."✳

✳ Keats in a letter to Benjamin Bailey
October 8, 1817

Hallmark → THE BEGINNING

CREATION OF ENTERPRISE

BARE facts:

Joyce Clyde Hall — Founder
- POOR BOY FROM NEBRASKA
- FULL OF ENERGY - COURAGE
  - AUDACITY
- COMMON SENSE/COMMON GENIUS
- TENACITY: "When you reach the end of your rope, tie a knot and <u>Hang on!</u>"

* HAD GOOD LUCK and BAD LUCK
   • PLAYED BOTH TO Advantage
   And built an EMPIRE
        ↓

(1910-1965)
55 years
× 365
——————
20,075 days

Hallmark Cards

⭐ ROMANTICIZING THE BARE FACTS:
The Beginning.

Well just look at that Country
Bumpkin — Joyce Clyde Hall
  fresh off the train
   from Norfolk, Nebraska,
     with fire in his heart
and a thermonuclear soul.

In a Twenty-thousand-day
     fit of passion
He fashioned blood,
   sweat,
     Tears,
       Gumption,
       ~~xxxxx~~ Genius,
         and Tenacity
INTO A GREAT AMERICAN
(business) DREAM
       ≡(HALLMARK)

"when you care enough to send the very best."

② Hallmark → MIDDLE AGE SETS IN

The ASCENT of FORMULA

Joyce Hall's initial DYNAMISM
      brought SUCCESS :★:
→ that success begot success formula
→ success formula begets ISOLATION

   (ISOLATION FROM **PASSION**
                    VISION
                    INVENTION)

      ISOLATION Begets: ATROPHY
                        DECAY
                        A FADING AWAY

"Old Enterprises never die, they
      just fade away."

   WHAT IF Hallmark could **DIE**
   instead of "just FADE AWAY?"

            ?

The Death of Enterprise → A FANTASY:

→ LISTEN!

Tic-Toc Tic-Toc Tic-Toc Tic-Toc ~~Tic-Toc~~
DEATH'S FOOTSTEPS.

Tic Toc
READY OR NOT

WHAT LIVES
DIES

ANIMAL,
VEGETABLE,
ENTERPRISE.

NO ESCAPE.
NOT EVEN THE WISE

NONE!
But One —

propagation!

Conceive of This:

A stratified
calcified
petrified
Enterprise
in desperation
forgoes ~~×~~ habitual cloning
and Tolerates
(allows)
permits
----genuine
birth

→

HOW TO ACHIEVE ENTREPRENEURIAL
IMMORTALITY
(A MESSAGE of Hope for aging Enterprise)

Propagate, Enterprise, propagate!
Have young!
Raise a family!
Put your offsprings' needs
ahead of your own.
Abuse them not
so they will not learn to abuse.

Inculcate values.

Then release your "Heirs of Enterprise"
To carry the torch as they see fit.

Old Enterprise,
You can then do
what the old do best:
Grow Wise
Die in peace
And let the cycle begin anew.

PROPAGATION IN THE DESERT:
(A poem -- sort of)

Behold! A great Pyramid
Mammoth blocks from solid rocks cut
with precision of edge & angle.
Each block ~~fits~~ fitted firmly against
its neighbors
In an enduring pattern of unmoving ~~fits~~
presence.

Picture deep within this monument to
reality past
A pocket of rich, damp loam
Where ~~Newn~~ Newness
(as yet undetected by corporate
weed pullers' dedication to extermination ~~~~
of any and all affronts to stone
tomb's barren ~~perfection~~ perfection)
. . . Germinates.
But, alas, ultimate detection is inevitable
And Newness,
Once discovered,
Will be pulled up by the roots ---
conscientiously.

And yet
What's this?
       A miracle!

This one time,
Newness, upon discovery, is spared
and allowed to take root--
            unmolested.

    Vulnerably,
       Tenderly,
    A shoot appears
    In a tentative
       Mystical
       Dance of creation.

    Yipes!
It grows not as a little pyramid,
    But as a Plum Tree!
Wonderous beyond the
       arid vocabulary
    of mere Pyramid Reality.

Lofty Pyramid watches
in scandalized indignation
But -- just this Once --
eschews to interfere.

Exquisite Freak!
Beautiful Mutation!
Awesome Newness!
You exist because Pyramid
-- this one time --
has found the grace to make room
for something other than
the narcissistic echoes
of its own remembered past.

You live because Pyramid
-- this one time --
has found the courage
to nurture something which has
the temerity to be unique.

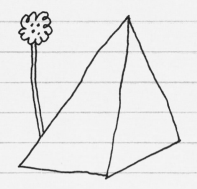

Little Plum tree,
    you are Newness
--- and Nowness.
Rooted in the tombs
    of Yesterday,
you bear the fruit
    that will see us through
        today.

CONVERSATIONS WITHIN THE PYRAMID ORGANIZATION!

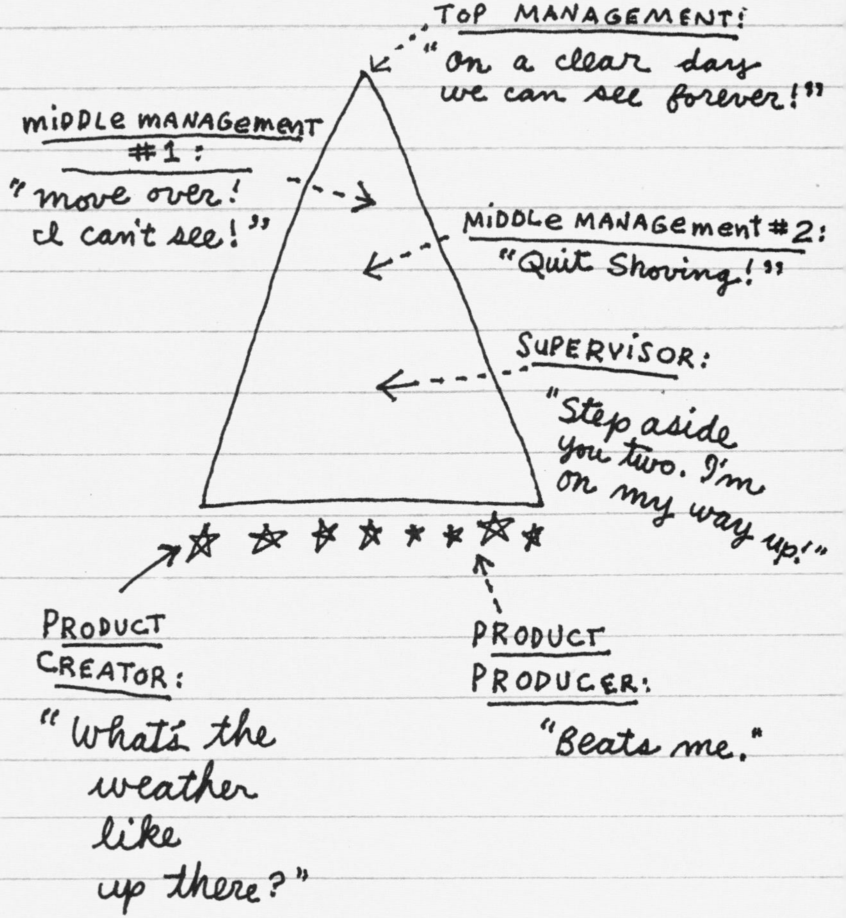

MORE PYRAMID TALK:

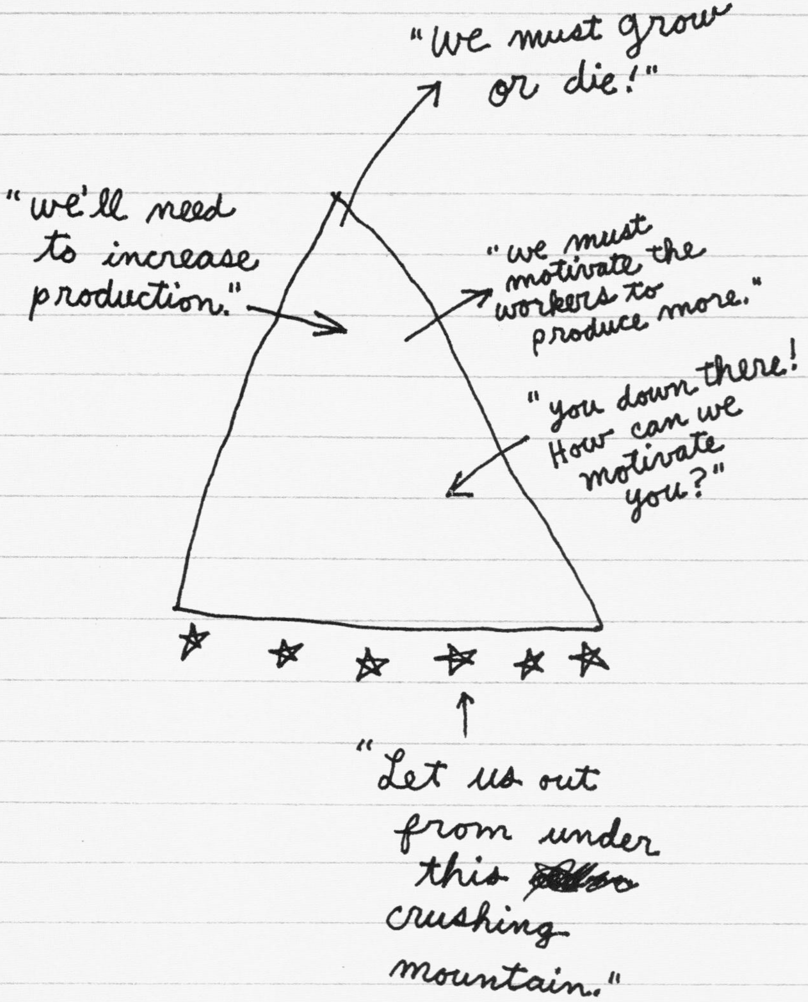

THE PLUM TREE
AS ORGANIZATIONAL MODEL:

product creators AND
product producers (the cash crop)
are at the top

MANAGERS and
SUPERVISORS
-- depicted as
~~branches~~ branches --
Exist to support
product
Producers

TOP
MANAGEMENT
-the trunk-
is the
enduring
central
support

CASH FLOW

PLUM TREE TALK:

PRODUCT
CREATORS: "on a clear day we can see forever."

"TOP" MANAGEMENT:
"what do you need to motivate you?"

"we've got what we need: sunshine and air."

CORPORATE RESOURCES FLOW UP FROM THE ROOTS TO MANAGEMENT and on up to product creators.

A SEMANTIC COMPARISON of PYRamid and PLUm TREE TERMINOLOGIES

A
PYRAMID

is a tomb

while

A
TREE

is a living organism

IN THE PYRAMID, THEY
ORGANIZE INTO

DIVISIONS

defined as "the state of being
divided"

IN THE PLUM TREE, THEY
ORGANIZE INTO

GROUPS

"a number of persons
who act as a unit"

much
more
positive
term ✓

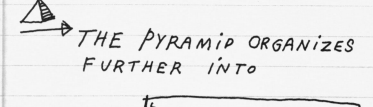 THE PYRAMID ORGANIZES
FURTHER INTO

DEPARTMENTS

defined as "major divisions
of a business"
(There's that Anti-unity word again)

THE PLUM TREE ORGANIZES
INTO VARIOUS

FORCES

"groups having the
Power of Effective action"

Positive!

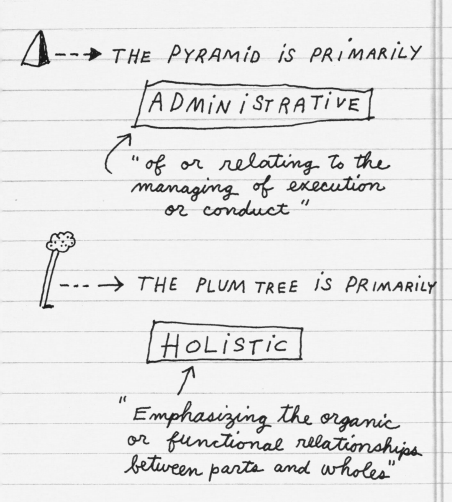

THE PYRAMID IS PRIMARILY

ADMINISTRATIVE

"of or relating to the managing of execution or conduct"

THE PLUM TREE IS PRIMARILY

HOLISTIC

"Emphasizing the organic or functional relationships between parts and wholes"

HALLMARK AS PYRAMID:

ADMINISTRATIVE ORGANIZATION

— function follows form —
(ie: FUNCTION follows organization)
eg: ediTorial and Design
are seen as separate functions
and are compartmentalized
into different departments,
(the blocks of the Pyramid)
this results in precise
organization charts
and the _death_ of
Natural Collaboration

This is
TRADITIONAL

Hallmark as PLUM TREE:

HOLISTIC ORGANIZATION

- form follows function
(ie: organization follows function)
eg: Editorial and design
are recognized as ~~they~~
two elements of the same
~~continuous~~ continuum and
so remain integrated
in a single creative
ecology rather than
hunkering down in separate
departments. This results
in an organic dynamism
and the enhancement
of collaboration.

↑
THIS IS
RADICAL

TRADITIONAL:

"The delivery of opinions, doctrines, practices, rites, and customs from generation to generation"

RADICAL:

"Going to the center, source, or foundation of something; fundemental; Basic."

★ (SO) → Radical would be a more fruitful approach than TRADITIONAL.

.. PLUM TREES are more ~~fruitful~~ bountiful than PYRAMIDS. △

I took all of these frenzied scribblings and massaged them into a presentation on the direction I thought Hallmark should go organizationally, more or less inviting management to come out of their pyramid and give birth to a plum tree.

I realized that the group I would be presenting to could be sensitive, defensive and sometimes combative. And many of the thoughts I intended to present could be taken as criticism of the way these people operated within Hallmark. So there seemed to me a real danger that many members of the audience would tune out, shut down or otherwise make themselves unavailable to much of what I planned to explore.

To avoid such a non-productive response, I chose a strategy of disarming foolishness. I opened my remarks by confessing that I was not qualified to discourse on so profound a subject as corporate organization and had, therefore, arranged for an outside consultant to take my place. As I launched into a lengthy introduction of our surprise (and fictitious) guest speaker, I produced an electric razor from behind the podium and shaved off my not insubstantial beard. Continuing, I donned a business shirt, tie and suit coat. I finished my costume change just as I concluded the introduction:

"Please join me in welcoming... Dr. Sheldon Watts."

I began to clap my hands and gestured toward the back of the room. To my amazement, everyone in the room turned in their chairs and began to applaud, also. This gave me a perfect opportunity to duck behind the podium and quickly put on a wig and switch to a pair of horn-rimmed eyeglasses.

"Thank you! Thank you!" an ebullient Dr. Watts responded, rising magically from behind the podium. He proceeded with his dissertation on pyramids and plum trees.

The audience's responses were beyond anything I could have hoped or imagined: They were raptly attentive throughout the entire presentation. And at the conclusion, when I removed my wig to become Gordon MacKenzie once again, I received an electrified standing ovation.

Blew me away!

We broke for coffee. I was surrounded by well wishers. I had *"opened a door and let the sunlight in,"* they said. This would surely prove to be *"a turning point in the way Hallmark operates."*

But the excitement faded over time, as it does. The pyramid did not go away. The Hairball remains; and Hallmark has stayed the course of its own destiny, as great corporations do.

The saving grace was that declaring my beliefs about the asphyxiating effects of mechanistic organization versus the vitalizing results of organic systems had an unexpected liberating effect on me. That experience of liberation through speaking my personal truths — along with the fact that my presentation caused no significant change of heart at Hallmark — convinced me that, in the future, my efforts would be best spent not in trying to change Hairballs, but in offering to midwife out of Hairballs anyone who longed for a fuller, more original work experience.

This then became my cardinal path — a path that, to this day, continues to bring me both adventure and soulful richness.

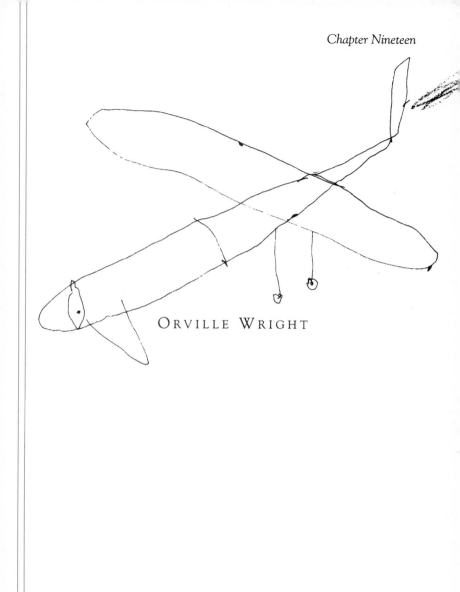

Chapter Nineteen

ORVILLE WRIGHT

Orville Wright did not have a pilot's license.

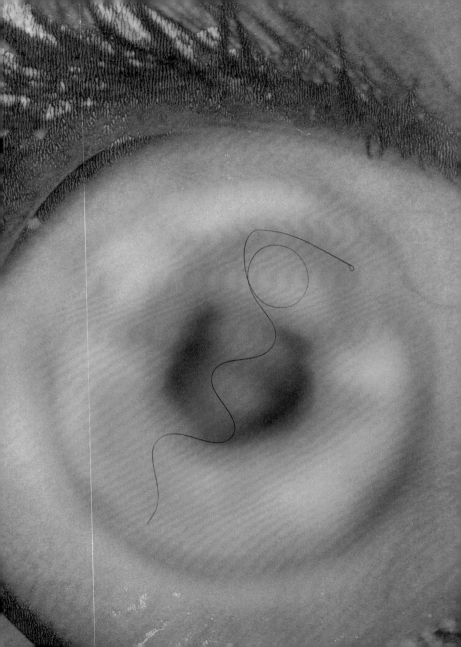

BEYOND MEASURE

En route from Shreveport, Louisiana, to San Jose, California.

Finished one workshop.

Headed for another.

Stuck on the tarmac at Dallas/Ft. Worth.

Our plane 16th in line for takeoff.

Waiting for a thunderstorm to pass.

Tired of reading, and having nothing better to do, I got to watching the little, hair-like things that float randomly across the surface of my eyeballs. Their behavior reminded me of the amorphous nature of creativity and a certain lack of appreciation of that amorphousness among the many corporations I visit. Perhaps I could use these little visual aberrations to illustrate a point for my clients. But first, in the name of prudence, I needed a quick reality check on the general awareness of these little optical squiggles.

Turning to the woman in the seat next to mine, I asked:

> *"Excuse me. Do you by any chance have little hair-like things floating across the surface of your eyeballs?"*

> *"What?! You, too?! Do you have those, too?! Oh! Ha-ha-ha! My God! I've had those things for years. But I've never wanted to say anything to anybody about them. I was afraid they'd think I was crazy!"*

So. Serendipity had brought my seatmate unexpected freedom to talk about something she had heretofore considered to be unmentionable. Now she was chatting affably about *"those lacy phantoms that glide to and fro"* across her field of vision.

"Those are vitreous floaters," interjected the man in the window seat on the other side of the woman. Turns out the newest member of our impromptu discussion group was a doctor, and he proceeded to give us the scientific view of the little squiggles.

The irresistible drama of the advancing thunderstorm distracted us from our conversation, and we each retreated into our own thoughts. But my fascination with vitreous floaters as metaphor for the nebulous nature of creativity remained.

Have you ever noticed:

If you look right at them — the squiggles, I mean — they go off to the side?

Right out of view if you keep staring at them.

And have you ever noticed, too, that, if you want them to return, all you have to do is stop looking at them? If you do that — stop looking at them — very gradually, they'll float back into your line of sight.

It's almost as if they're shy.

Stare at them, and they'll go away.

Look the other way, and, silently, they will reappear.

Shy.

Creativity is like that. It will not be looked at. As soon as you look at creativity — as soon as you become conscious (or self-conscious) of it — it simply vanishes.

If you want it to return, you must give up trying to focus on it.

But, because you cannot focus on it, you cannot measure the actual creative process. Well, in the eyes of any Anal Retentive worth his salt, anything that cannot be measured is of doubtful value — and even of doubtful existence.

No surprise then that the Anal Retentives, as Trustees of the Hairball, are loath to commit resources or genuine moral support to the amorphous concept of creativity. They lust for the *fruits* of creativity (especially when they see the very measurable results of a successful competitor's creative efforts) but mistrust the *act* of creativity, which remains invisible and elusive.

Only the Renegades in Orbit, removed from the Hairball's obsession with quantifying everything, are free to reap the unpredictable bounty of the inscrutable creative process.

If an organization wishes to benefit from its own creative potential, it must be prepared to value the vagaries of the unmeasurable as well as the certainties of the measurable.

Chapter Twenty-One

A CONFERENCE OF ANGELS

Typically, Ambassador Cards, a subsidiary of Hallmark, holds annual regional sales conferences at strategic locations across the country. Like sales meetings anywhere, a major purpose of the events is to spur the field people on — for the continued prosperity of all.

One year, I was asked to sit in on the task force assembled from around the country to plan the next scheduled conferences. My role was first to observe the proceedings of the group and then to facilitate an ideation session aimed at generating concepts for new conference formats.

The task force met at 8:00 one morning. The centerpiece of their dreary conference room was that altar of numbers worshippers, the overhead projector. It was immediately put to use. To the accompaniment of the projector's droning fan, task force members took turns fussing with transparencies of unreadable charts and sleep-inducing columns of figures, all of which were eventually projected onto a plain wall serving as a projection screen.

"You guys are dead in the water," I thought but did not say.

Gathered to create excitement, the group was, instead, oozing into a stupor of statistics. *(So soon!)*

It took forever for coffee break to arrive. When it did, the room emptied fast, people making a beeline, first for the rest rooms and then down the hall to the beverage machines, which are set to dispense free drinks at certain times in the midmorning and midafternoon. (Another of Hallmark's generous benefits — caffeine for the cause.)

I waylaid the woman who had originally asked me to join the group.

"Is it always like this? I don't think this is working."

She grinned blankly.

201.

"May I try something different for the brainstorm?"

"Uh... Oh... Kay..."

That's all I needed. With a rush of excitement, I dashed to my room on the floor above. Time was short. Coffee break would end soon, and the task force would be shuffling back into its dismal chamber. I rummaged through the clutter under my drawing board till I found what I was looking for — a handful of small candles of the type used to keep fondue pots warm and a pair of Tibetan cymbals. Clutching these magic props, I hurried, puffing, back to the conference room just in time to sweep away the overhead projector and replace it with the small candles, which I set randomly along the length of the conference table.

The ritualistic coffee-break chatter about the past weekend's football games faded to an uncertain silence as the task force, filing back into the room, eyed me lighting the half-dozen candles. The muffled shuffling of the group reseating itself only served to underline the new silence. People were exchanging sidelong glances in search of some clue as to what the hell was going on, but nobody asked. Every face had become remarkably expressionless. I spoke in as reassuring a tone as I could muster:

> *"The other day, I met a man who spoke to me of empty mind.*
> *And although I'm not clear on all he said, I came away with*
> *the awareness that if we are to make ourselves available to*
> *what our vast unconscious has to offer us, we must first empty*
> *the hoppers of our conscious minds. We must make room."*

I produced the cymbals, two shallow-dished bronze disks measuring two-and-three-quarter inches in diameter, both tied to opposite ends of a foot-long leather thong.

> *"These are Tibetan Tingshas. When I was first introduced to them, I was told they are cast from eight of the trace elements that exist naturally in the human body. Perhaps as a result, their resonating ring is remarkably calming.*

> *"What I'd like to do now is turn off the overhead lights so we are sitting in soft candlelight. And then I'm going to ring the cymbals. I would ask you to close your eyes. Relax. And let the sound of the bells wash over you."*

Someone turned the lights out. I took the cymbals by the thong, holding it in both hands in front of me so the bronze discs hung about three inches from each other, just below my eye level. I shifted my hands apart and then toward each other. The cymbals struck. A tone of exquisite clarity caressed the silence of the room. I rang them again. Their note, though inevitably fading slowly to inaudibility, was the sound of eternity.

Twelve angels in business suits sat serenely in the candles' glow.

I rang the bells a third time. As their sound ebbed once again, I quietly intoned:

> *"Picture in your mind's eye a small and delicate flower*

> *Floating gently inside your skull,*

> *Just behind the bone of your forehead.*

> *Notice the flower's color,*

> *Its shape,*

The pattern of its petals.

Let the flower drift slowly downward,

Gliding gently down your throat into your rib cage.

Drifting down and down...

Between your lungs... downward, gently downward,

Coming to rest in the lowest place in your abdomen

Where your breath reaches

When you breathe fully and deeply.

A quiet touch of color deep in the darkness of your abdomen.

Hold the flower there... hold it... hold it...

Now:

Let it go!

Let the flower vanish.

But stay focused on the place where it was

Deep down in the dark center of you."

We sat in silence for about 90 seconds, which is a very long time for busy business people.

"Now, when you're ready... only when you're ready... open your eyes and come back into the room."

More silence. Then, here and there, people began to open their eyes. There was a peace in the room that had not been there before.

"I'm going to turn the lights back on now. Sorry about that."

The glare of fluorescent ceiling lights intruded back into the room.
The angels moaned in protest. I continued:

*"You have just experienced 'letting go.' Please accept the idea
that when you let go of the flower you also let go of any
notions or biases you held about where you thought this meeting
would or should go.*

*"Now, if you would, please feed me. Call out everything
you've ever hated about any sales meeting you've ever attended.
I'll write it all down on this flip chart."*

We filled six pages.

*"Now, building on these negatives, create a sales meeting format
that rises above them all."*

The group exploded. The shell of their corporate reserve split open,
and a breathtaking flood of pent-up, common-sense know-how
transformed their arid, grey conference room into a cauldron of creativity.
Eagerness, enthusiasm, optimism filled the air. Everyone threw ideas
on the table with joyous abandon. People were listening, seizing others'
ideas and vaulting to the next plateau. I slipped out of the room,
chortling at the mischief that had just been unleashed.

The task force went on to create a regional sales meeting format
that was unlike any the company had ever considered before. I heard
later that it made upper management very nervous. But, to their credit,
they stood aside and let the task force develop an event that excited
the enthusiasm of every sales region across the country and engaged
the people in the field to a degree unparalleled. Before or since.

What had happened at that first task force meeting? Well, I think the group's initial fixation on statistical anchors — via the static medium of the overhead projector — was in step with the analysis-oriented corporate norm. In obsessing over the history represented by their statistics, the group was being *culturally* appropriate. But it was being *functionally* inappropriate, because the goal of the meeting was *supposed* to have been to create new sales meeting concepts. And creating something new is *genesis,* which comes *before* history.

To be functionally inappropriate is to be dysfunctional. One way past this dysfunction was to give the meeting attenders (through the unorthodoxy of candles, bells, and guided imagery presented in a non-threatening way) permission to escape from the Hairball of their history and move into a nebulous alternate reality — the Orbit of genesis where to create is the norm.

Release from their inculcated culture allowed the task force members to metamorphize — for a little while — from mere attendants at a meeting into vibrant participants in an evolving endeavor.

The escape from habitual culture must always be temporary if you wish to be permitted back into that culture...

> *"Yes, you may go out and play; but you must be home by dinner time."*

However, temporary as these Orbits out of the Hairball may be, they are expeditions that promise finding in the chaos beyond culture antidotes for the stagnation of status quo.

Chapter Twenty-Two

DYNAMIC FOLLOWING

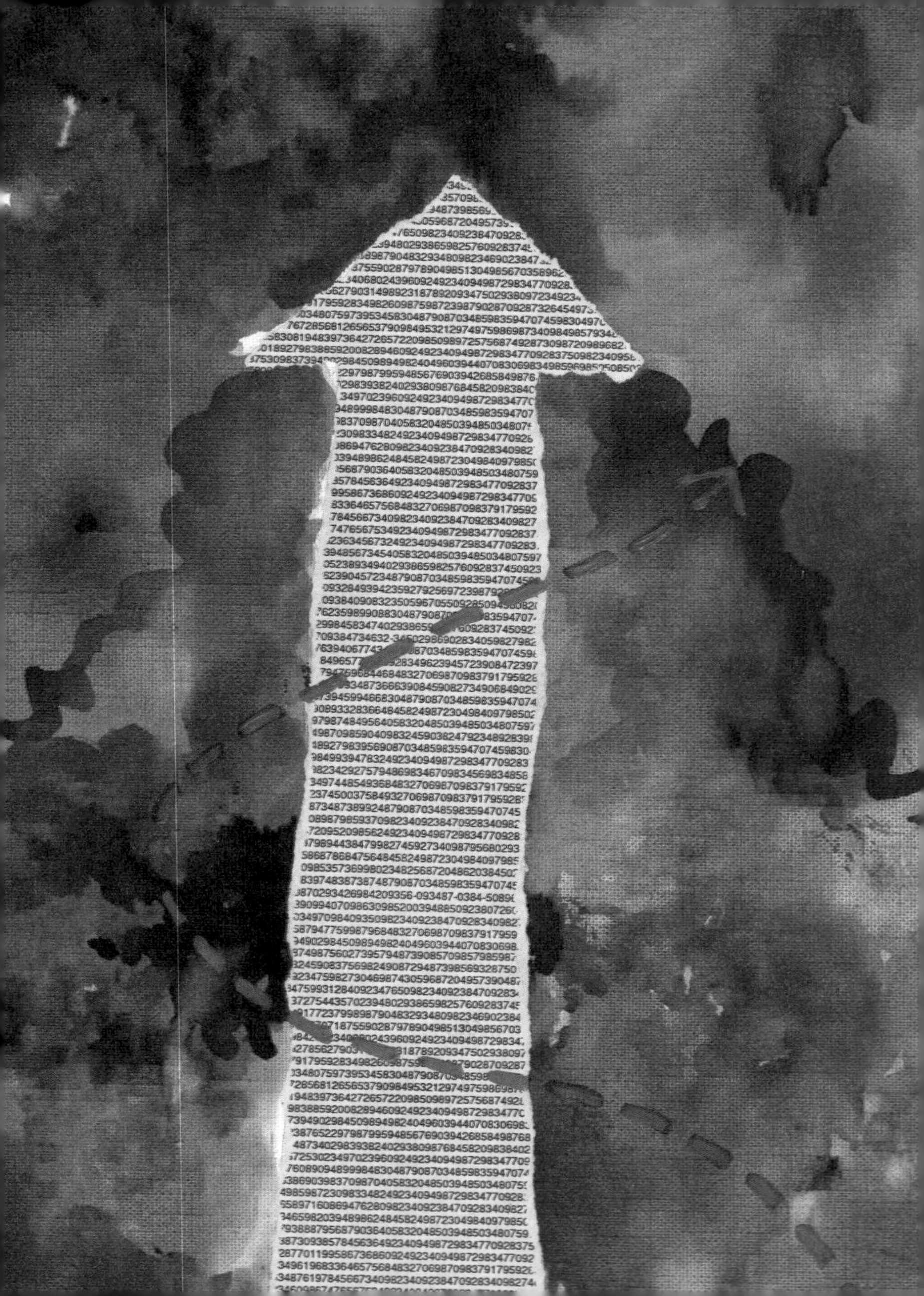

If we were to think of waterskiing as a metaphor for leading and following, the person at the wheel, in the boat, dry, would represent the leader. And the skier in the water, wet, would be the follower.

Wherever the leader goes, the follower goes. If, for reasons unknown to the follower, the leader decides to steer the boat through an area where clusters of reeds are growing up out of the water, about three feet tall, the reaction of the follower might be:

"Why are we goin' over there?

"This is gonna hurt.

"And it's gonna hurt me, not you!"

If you are a skier in this situation, you have at least a couple of options other than being whipped painfully through the reeds.

Option #1:

You can let go of the towline. Become an entrepreneur — on your own, in the middle of the lake.

Option #2:

You can become a better waterskier. Learn to ski out beyond the confines of the boat's wake, way 'round to the right, thus dodging some of the threatening reeds. Then, describing a great, broad arc, ski back over the wake, over the wake again and way 'round to the left, avoiding more reeds.

Every point on the arc
is a point of *legitimate following.*

During the latter part of my career at Hallmark, because I didn't seem to have anything much to do, people felt free to come and visit me from time to time. As often as not, they simply wanted to unload. It is a fact of our current corporate cultures that more "stuff" is continually dumped on us. Day after day after day. To ease the ordeal of our ever-growing burdens, it sometimes helps to find someone to unload on. Well, not really unload on. Unload *in front of* would be more accurate. To find someone who is willing to witness our usually hidden corporate pain. Many Hallmarkers found that witness in me.

When these visits first started, I was not ready for them. I had a deep compulsion to control. As someone would begin to open up to me, my knee-jerk reaction would be to try to fix whatever predicament they were describing.

Or I would try to fix *the person*. Invariably, I could fix neither. It always ended badly. People would leave with a sense of not having been heard, and I would be left with a sense of helplessness (not a pleasant feeling for a control freak).

Then, in the course of my efforts to develop spiritually, I happened to be reading an article on Vipassana meditation. In it the author wrote about achieving a state of "compassionate emptiness."

Compassionate emptiness. The two words seized me and would not let go. *Compassionate emptiness.* To me that meant a state of nonjudgmental receiving. I thought:

> "I will try to be in that state when people come to me to recount their burdens."

From that day on, whenever somebody would come by to pour out their company woes, I would *listen.* In silence.

I would imagine myself to be an empty vessel existing only to receive. As fully as possible. Without judgment.

Interestingly, when I stopped interfering with their process, many of my visitors — those who were ready — would begin to come up with solutions of their own. And, when we would part company, each of us would be the better for the experience.

Although I would sit in silence most of the time during these sessions, there were occasions when verbal intervention seemed appropriate. One of those times would be whenever anyone said:
  "I wish we had more dynamic leadership around here."

I would respond:
  "I wish we had more dynamic following around here. That's where the real energy of an organization comes from."

My last boss at Hallmark, a fellow by the name of Bob Kipp, sat at the wheel of one of the corporate speedboats. I was at the end of a towline on waterskis. We spent our time together skimming across great Lake Hallmark. Kipp was so sure of who he was and why he was where he was and where the power was that he was not threatened at all when I would ski around in a wide arc until I was up even with the boat and sometimes even past it. He knew I was not going to start pulling the boat with him in it. It just doesn't work that way. The power remains in the boat. But, in allowing me to ski past him — in a sense, allowing me to lead — he would unleash in me an excitement about our enterprise that served our shared goals well.

If you are in a position of power and want to lead well, remember:

Allow those *you* lead...

To lead... when they feel the need.

All will benefit.

Chapter Twenty-Three

POOL-HALL DOG

On my way to a conference in Stevens Point, Wisconsin, feeling a little hungry — it was near noon — I spotted an invitingly funky-looking roadside restaurant and pulled in. After ordering a cheeseburger and diet cola, I scanned, with idle interest, the floor-to-ceiling clutter of local memorabilia that served as interior decor. Eventually, my wandering gaze carried me to two pool tables on the far side of the room beyond the eating area. One table was in use; the other was not. Beneath the vacant table, I saw a dog's legs. Standing. Still. I continued to scan the room, but with less interest than before. My eyes kept returning to the dog legs: still still.

My cheeseburger came. I ate without tasting. Distracted, transfixed really, by the motionless legs. I started feeling a little uneasy. Surely the dog was not stuffed... like the sad heads of moose and deer staring out from the cafe walls. That would be going too far. (*"Strange,"* I'd thought, *"Stuffed moose is okay; stuffed dog is not."*) But the legs remained motionless. How repugnant! A stuffed dog. I was regretting ever having entered such a grotesque establishment when, to my relief, the dog's tail moved — ever so slightly.

> *"Oh, good. I was mistaken. It's not a stuffed dog, after all.*
> *Just my imagination running rampant."*

The tail moved again, a subtle wag. Done eating, I could not leave without investigating what curious circumstances might keep this half-hidden dog standing still for so long. I paid my check and walked over to the other side of the pool tables.

Do you know how, along the side or end of some pool tables, there is a slot or trough where the balls go when they're sunk? Well, this dog had reached his mouth into the trough of the pool table and locked his jaws around one of the sunken balls. No way was he about to let go of his prize — but neither could he remove his mouth. His jaws,

opened wide to accommodate the ball, were consequently opened too wide to allow him to escape from the confines of the trough. So there he stood, dead still, except for the now-and-then, hope-against-hope wag of his tail.

I turned to the men absorbed in their play at the other table:

"Look at that dog!"

"Oh, he does that all the time," responded one player.

"I've seen him stand like that for over an hour sometimes," added the other. *"He wants someone to play with him."*

Poor dog. I left the restaurant feeling both sad for the mutt and fascinated by the lesson he'd provided:

> *If we do not let go, we make prisoners of ourselves.*

To be fully free to create, we must first find the courage and willingness to let go:

Let go of the strategies that have worked for us in the past...

Let go of our biases, the foundation of our illusions...

Let go of our grievances, the root source of our victimhood...

Let go of our so-often-denied fear of being found unlovable.

You will find it is not a one-shot deal, this letting go. You must do it again and again and again. It's kind of like breathing. You can't breathe just once. Try it: Breathe just once. You'll pass out.

If you stop letting go, your creative spirit will pass out.

Now when I say *let go,* I do not mean *reject.* Because when you let go of something, it will still be there for you when you need it. But because you have stopped clinging, you will have freed yourself up to tap into other possibilities — possibilities that can help you deal with this world of accelerating change.

Chapter Twenty-Four

PAINT ME A MASTERPIECE

In your mind, conjure an image of the Mona Lisa. Visualize that masterpiece's subtleties of hue and tone as clearly as you can.

Next, shift to the image of a paint-by-numbers Mona Lisa. Envision the flat, raw colors meeting hard-edged, one against the other.

Now, let me relate a fantasy about masterpieces, paint-by-numbers and you. It goes like this:

Before you were born, God came to you and said:

HI, THERE! I JUST DROPPED BY TO WISH
YOU LUCK. AND TO ASSURE YOU
THAT   YOU AND I WILL
BE   MEETING   AGAIN.
SOON. BEFORE YOU KNOW IT.

YOU'RE HEADING OUT ON AN ADVENTURE
THAT WILL BE FILLED WITH FASCINATING
EXPERIENCES. YOU'LL START OUT AS A
TINY   SPECK   FLOATING   IN   AN
I   N   F   I   N   I   T   E   ,
DARK OCEAN, QUITE SATURATED
WITH NUTRIENTS. SO YOU WON'T
HAVE   TO GO LOOKING FOR
FOOD OR A JOB OR   ANYTHING
LIKE THAT. ALL YOU'LL HAVE TO DO IS
FLOAT IN THE DARKNESS.

AND GROW   INCREDIBLY.

          AND CHANGE MIRACULOUSLY.

YOU'LL SPROUT ARMS AND LEGS.

AND HANDS AND FEET.

AND FINGERS AND TOES.

AS IF FROM NOTHING, YOUR HEAD WILL TAKE FORM. YOUR NOSE, YOUR MOUTH, YOUR EYES AND EARS WILL EMERGE.

AS YOU CONTINUE TO GROW BIGGER AND BIGGER, YOU WILL BECOME AWARE THAT THIS DARK, OCEANIC ENVIRONMENT OF YOURS — WHICH, WHEN YOU WERE TINY, SEEMED SO VAST IS NOW ACTUALLY CRAMPED AND CONFINING. THAT WILL LEAD YOU TO THE UNAVOIDABLE CONCLUSION THAT YOU'RE GOING TO HAVE TO MOVE TO A BIGGER PLACE.

AFTER MUCH GROPING ABOUT IN THE DARK, YOU WILL FIND AN EXIT. THE MOUTH OF A TUNNEL.

"TOO SMALL," YOU'LL DECIDE. "COULDN'T POSSIBLY SQUEEZE THROUGH THERE."

BUT THERE WILL BE NO OTHER APPARENT WAY OUT. SO, WITH PRIMAL SPUNK, YOU WILL TAKE ON YOUR FIRST "IMPOSSIBLE" CHALLENGE AND ENTER THE TUNNEL.

IN DOING SO, YOU WILL BE EMBARKING ON A BRUTAL, NO-TURNING-

BACK, PHYSICALLY EXHAUS+ING,
CLAUS+R⊕PH⊕BIC PASSAGE + H A +
WILL IN+R⊕DUCE Y⊕U +⊕ PAIN AND
FEAR AND HARD PHYSICAL LAB⊕R.
I+ WILL SEEΠ +⊕ +AKE F⊕REVER.
BU+ ΠYS+ERI⊕US UNDULA+I⊕NS ⊕ F
+HE +UNNEL I+SELF WILL HELP
SQUIRΠ Y⊕U +HR⊕UGH. AND FINALLY,
AF+ER WHA+ WILL SEEΠ LIKE
IN+ERΠINABLE S + R I V I N G , Y⊕U
WILL BREAK +HR⊕UGH +⊕ A
BLINDING LIGH+.

GIAN+ HANDS WILL PULL Y⊕U
GEN+LY, BU+ FIRΠLY,
IN+⊕ AN E N ⊕ R Π ⊕ U S
R⊕⊕Π. THERE WILL BE
SEVERAL HUGE PE⊕PLE, CALLED
ADUL+S, HUDDLING AR⊕UND Y⊕U, AS
IF +⊕ GREE+ Y⊕U. IF I+ IS AN ⊕LD-
FASHI⊕NED PLACE, ⊕NE ⊕F + H E S E
H U Π ⊕ N G ⊕ U S PE⊕PLE
ΠAY H⊕LD Y⊕U UPSIDE D⊕WN BY
+HE LEGS AND GIVE Y⊕U A SWA+
⊕N +HE BACKSIDE +⊕ GE+ Y⊕U G⊕ING.

ALL ⊕F +HIS WILL BE WHA+ +HE BIG
PE⊕PLE ⊕N +HE ⊕+HER SIDE
CALL BEING B⊕RN. F⊕R Y⊕U, I+ WILL
BE ⊕NLY +HE FIRS+ ⊕F Y⊕UR
NEW LIFE'S ΠANY EXPL⊕I+S.

God continues:

> I WAS WONDERING, WHILE YOU'RE
>   OVER THERE ON THE OTHER SIDE,
> WOULD YOU   DO ME A FAVOR?

"*Sure!*" you chirp.

> WOULD YOU TAKE THIS ARTIST'S
> CANVAS WITH YOU AND PAINT A
> MASTERPIECE FOR ME?   I'D REALLY
> APPRECIATE
>
>   THAT.

Beaming, God hands you a pristine canvas. You roll it up, tuck it under your arm and head off on your journey.

Your birth is just as God had predicted, and when you come out of the tunnel into the bright room, some doctor or nurse looks down at you in amazement and gasps:

  "*Look! The little kid's carrying a rolled-up artist's canvas!*"

Knowing that you do not yet have the skills to do anything meaningful with your canvas, the big people take it away from you and give it to society for safekeeping until you have acquired the prescribed skills requisite to the canvas's return. While society is holding this property of yours, it cannot resist the temptation to unroll the canvas and draw pale blue lines and little blue numbers all over its virgin surface. Eventually, the canvas is returned to you, its rightful owner. However, it now carries the implied message that if you will paint inside the blue lines and follow the instructions of the little blue numbers your life will be a masterpiece.

5

4

And that is a lie.   **12**

For more than 50 years I worked on my paint-by-numbers creation. With uneven but persistent diligence, I dipped an emaciated paint-by-numbers brush into color No. 1 and painstakingly painted inside each little blue-bordered area marked 1. Then on to 2 and 3 and 4 and so on. Sometimes, during restive periods of my life, I would paint, say, the 12 spaces before the 10 spaces (a token rebellion against overdoses of linearity). More than once, I painted beyond a line and, feeling embarrassed, would either try to wipe off the errant color or cover it over with another before anyone might notice my lack of perfection. From time to time, although not often, someone would compliment me, unconvincingly, on the progress of my "masterpiece." I would gaze at the richness of others' canvases. Doubt about my own talent for painting gnawed at me. Still, I continued to fill in the little numbered spaces, unaware of, or afraid to look at, any real alternative.

Then there came a time, after half a century of daubing more or less inside the lines, that my days were visited by traumatic events. The dividends of my noxious past came home to roost, and the myth of my life began horrifically to come unglued. I pulled back from my masterpiece-in-the-works and saw it with an emerging clarity.

It looked awful.

The stifled strokes of paint had nothing to do with me. They did not illustrate who I am or speak of whom I could become. I felt duped, cheated, ashamed — anguished that I had wasted so much canvas, so much paint. I was angry that I had been conned into doing so.

But that is the past. Passed.

Today I wield a wider brush — pure ox-bristle. And I'm swooping it through the sensuous goo of Cadmium Yellow, Alizarin Crimson or Ultramarine Blue (not Nos. 4, 13 or 8) to create the biggest, brightest, funniest, fiercest damn dragon that I can. Because that has more to do with what's inside of me than some prescribed plagiarism of somebody else's *tour de force*.

You have a masterpiece inside you, too, you know. One unlike any that has ever been created, or ever will be.

And remember:

> If you go to your grave
>
> without painting
>
> your masterpiece,
>
> it will not
>
> get painted.
>
> No one else
>
> can paint it.

> *Only you.*

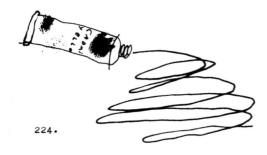